TEACHING PEACE

TEACHING PEACE

A Restorative Justice Framework for Strengthening Relationships

∞ § ∞

Beverly B. Title, Ph.D.

This book comes to you courtesy of
ReSolutionaries, Inc. to provide support for your
school's work with restorative justice practices. We thank
you for empowering our children and youth with the tools to
build a better, more peaceful world. - *Beverly B.Title*

www.resolutionariesinc.com

TEACHING PEACE: A Restorative Justice Framework for Strengthening Relationships

Published by Del Hayes Press, 1690 Estates Parkway, Allen, TX 75002. 972-727-3693. First edition. Visit our website at www.delhayespress.com.

ISBN-13: 978-0-9822706-4-6
ISBN-10: 0-9822706-4-x

Cover design: Ward Flynn and Dylan Dickey
Text design: Stephanie Brooks

For permissions or requests, contact the author:
Beverly B. Title, Ph. D
P. O. Box 273
Lafayette, CO 80226
Beverly@resolutionariesinc.com

Printed in the United States of America

Del Hayes Press

Dedication

To my child and her children, and their children and their children's children. May they never forget to remember the ancient teachings of the peacemakers.

∞§∞

In Remembrance

The restorative justice community owes much to Dennis Maloney. He inspired us with his wisdom, his kindness, his eloquence and his tenacious fight for what's right. We miss you, Denny. You live on in our hearts and in our practice of restorative justice.

A portion of the profits from this book is being donated to the Longmont Community Justice Partnership to further the work of restorative justice.

*"True peace is not merely the absence of tension.
It is the presence of Justice."*

— M. L. King, Jr.

Contents

Index of Stories

Preface

The English language presented some ethical challenges in writing this book. I elected to forego the standard grammatical practice of masculine pronoun use, and instead opted for the random use of masculine and feminine forms. The practice of masculine usage is antiquated, and I ask that modern grammarians resolve this issue. Language is powerful, and our society would be better served by forms that reflect egalitarian values and promote gender equity. Furthermore, I have chosen to capitalize the word Circle to honor it as a proper place, or proper noun.

Throughout our practice of restorative justice at the Longmont Community Justice Partnership since 1996, we have worked closely with the criminal justice system. Despite repeated and earnest effort, we have not yet been able to move away fully from the language of that system, although we recognize that it does not reflect the values of restorative justice. Terms like "victim" and "offender" are labels and do not honor the value of the person behind the label. Those terms are used in this book to refer to "roles" in the restorative process, but they are not terms to use with a real person. In those cases, it is best to use the person's name.

The following quote from *Dancing with a Ghost; exploring Indian reality* by Rupert Ross[1] is offered. Ross quotes an Ojibway elder talking about his similar struggles with the English language.

> *... Ojibway was a 'softer' language than English when it came to describing such things. Ojibway did not contain expressions for such concepts as 'the accused' or 'the offender,' concepts which have the effect of stigmatizing the person involved. Ojibway terms, he told me, would not amount to 'labels' like our words would, for they would not characterize the person but describe, in gentle terms, what he or she had done. They were verb-oriented expressions, not*

iii

categorizing nouns, and as such they do not 'freeze' a person within a particular classification for the rest of his life. With their emphasis on activity, these words instead emphasize process rather than state, thus helping the person who hears them to understand that all of life is a process and every person is a 'thing-which-is-becoming.' As opposed to a 'thing-which-is.' From this perspective, no one can be written off because of what they did at a particular moment in time. Instead, since each person is always 'someone-in-the-making,' it becomes everyone's duty to assist in that process.

Acknowledgements

My appreciation goes to Spirit and all her assistants, the family, friends, and others on my path who have loved me enough to tell me the truth, the sweet truths and the hard truths, that have helped me become a better human.

A special gratitude for those who have thoroughly believed in me, who held the dream of Teaching Peace and helped me live it: Lana, David and Summer; Mike Butler, Jen Brown, Deb Witzel and all the many staff and volunteers who manifested its dream; Lana Leonard and Linda Leary for their immense help capturing the stories, and to Ana Arias for reflection and guidance. Thanks also to Stephanie Brooks for her meticulous attention to detail and formatting assistance.

Further gratitude is offered for Kappy Hall, my partner in ReSolutionaries, Inc., for her editorial support and assistance in the refinement of this book and for the ways in which her thinking and our discussions have contributed to my understanding of restorative practices.

In the 1990's and early 2000's the restorative justice movement found its way to Colorado. We owe a huge debt of gratitude to the Colorado Forum on Community Restorative Justice and Anne Rogers for their role in convening practitioners and bringing excellent people to teach and inspire us. Among those who advanced restorative practices in Colorado are Dennis Maloney, Kay Pranis, Mark Umbreit, Howard Zehr, Mark Carey, Gordon Bazemore, Mara Schiff, Anne Seymour and Ted Wachtel. Look at all the positive ripples you have inspired in Colorado!

A special appreciation is offered for my longtime friend, Lisa Eringen, for the many gifts she brought to my life and her constant encouragement to write this book. If there is wisdom in this book, it is because so many have contributed so much.

Time Line

1994 – Beverly Title and Lana Leonard founded Teaching Peace as a nonprofit agency dedicated to violence prevention.

1996 – Longmont Community Justice Partnership was created as a program of Teaching Peace. It was organized as a partnership among the Longmont, (Colorado) Police Department and Municipal Court, the St. Vrain Valley School District, Alternatives for Youth, and Teaching Peace which serves as the managing partner.

2010 – Longmont Community Justice Partnership (LCJP) replaced Teaching Peace as the name for the nonprofit organization.

Introduction

This book is about the experience of bringing restorative justice to one community through an organization named Teaching Peace and what was learned along the way. It clarifies the meaning of the restorative approach to justice, and chronicles some of our triumphs and challenges in doing that work. It also suggests a guide for living our day-to-day lives in a way that brings happiness and well-being based on the principles and values that are foundational to restorative justice. It tells the stories of our experiences with those who had committed crimes and those who were impacted by the offenses.

Restorative justice, at the simplest level, may be understood as bringing together the people most impacted by a crime or conflict to decide together what harm has been done and how that harm may be repaired. It has become a worldwide movement that is gaining momentum because of its intrinsic appeal and consistently strong outcomes. Across lines of culture and class, people around the globe respond positively when they hear about restorative justice.

"Why aren't we doing this all the time, everywhere?" is a common question I hear when presenting the restorative way. Some countries, like Australia and England, are making great strides in reforming their criminal justice and school discipline systems through restorative lenses. In our community of Longmont and the state of Colorado, we are making some headway in this direction. In the last few years the Colorado legislature has passed bills to endorse restorative justice and have created a statewide council to promote its use. Despite these positive steps, the legislature has not yet taken the most critical one of allocating dollars specifically for restorative justice. I am hopeful this will come soon and multiply the good that the restorative process brings. As an appointed member of that state council, I invite you to track and support our progress at www.rjcolorado.org.

This book is an anthem, sung brave and bold, that is only possible because of the dedicated life force of hundreds of people in our community and millions of others around the world. It is a tribute to them. Many of us were initially motivated toward restorative justice by wanting to provide a response to crime and violence that was intrinsically whole and offered an opportunity for healing *all* involved parties. We recognize that punishment, even when imparted with the best of intentions, focuses on balancing the pain rather than restoring the loss, and it often brings unwanted side effects.

For fifteen years I worked as an alternative school teacher, with many students who were in my class when they were not in jail. These youth were beautiful spirits caught up in challenging life circumstances which they often responded to violently. From them I learned that punishment is often internalized as another form of violence done to them, leaving them feeling entitled to "return the favor." Through those years, I came to see our jails as crime colleges where people learn better criminal skills and come out more angry, having experienced deeper levels of hurt, and, therefore, feeling justified in causing more pain to others. And for this, we pay their tuition! My work with these students taught me there were more effective ways to address "mis"behavior, ways that bring greater understanding and connectedness with others. Restorative justice is particularly brilliant at building those bonds of connection. So when I encountered restorative justice, there was no turning back. I was compelled to bring it to my community.

> **Through those years, I came to see our jails as crime colleges where people learn better criminal skills and come out more angry.**

Restorative justice rests on a foundation of values and principles. These tenets may be implemented in any number of ways that generally involve a circle of people exploring a wrong or conflict with the focus on repairing harm and making things right to the greatest extent possible. An internet search of restorative justice values and principles will reveal hundreds of sources, as much is written on this topic. In an effort to provide a concise version for our volunteers that is fairly easy to recall, I began to articulate the R's. The first version contained 4 R's with Reintegration, the fifth R, being added later. The sequence of the R's varied in earlier versions. Over the years, the scope and sequence have become precise. The 5 R's are: Relationship, Respect, Responsibility, Repair, and Reintegration. Since our volunteer team has over a hundred people at times who are doing this work, it was important that we be consistent in our service delivery. The 5 R's are taught to everyone; they were the code to live by and turn to as the basis for all decision making.

Our team of community of practitioners started out believing that we were doing this work as a service to our community and to the offenders and crime victims and their families that we touched. After a couple short years, we began to understand the depth to which our own lives had been impacted by this work. As a community of restorative justice practitioners, we realized and discussed the extent to which we were living our lives more clearly, more directly, more specifically guided by the values and principles of our restorative justice work. The 5 R's became not only the umbrella for our volunteer work, but also the guide for raising our children, enhancing our marriages and interacting with our neighbors. We realized that the 5 R's had, in fact, become a way of life.

> **The 5 R's became not only the umbrella for our volunteer work, but also the guide for raising our children, enhancing our marriages and interacting with our neighbors. We realized that the 5 R's had, in fact, become a way of life.**

Restorative justice practitioners are fond of saying, "Just trust the process." We have witnessed the remarkable outcomes that come from letting the magic of the Circle do its work. It sounds a bit woo-woo even to me, so I do not expect you, dear reader, to accept that yet; however, I suspect you may as we walk together through the experiences that led us to this conclusion. You may come to understand the depth of these 5 basic principles: Relationship, Respect, Responsibility, Repair, and Reintegration. You may even glimpse their capacity to enrich your life.

This book is intended for those who are curious about restorative justice and want to understand what the buzz is about. It may be useful to anyone who has not found justice in the justice system and is looking for another path to peace. It is intended for parents, grandparents, teachers and anyone else with responsibility for children, who can appreciate a basic set of principles to assist them to do their job well and to pass along to those children as guideposts for life. This book is offered to people who work in the criminal justice system and diligently carry the responsibility and the frustration of trying to make that system work; I hope you will find some examples of restorative language that may be useful to you. In reading the LCJP story, I hope my fellow restorative justice practitioners will be inspired to more deeply connect with the work and with our worldwide RJ family. This book is written for all the peacemakers who are trying to help themselves and others find new tools that consistently work to resolve conflict and restore damaged relationships. It is offered in tribute to the indigenous ones who conceived the restorative way, to shed light on their wisdom that is so dearly needed in our modern time.

I have interspersed many stories to illustrate and emphasize the points made in the book. There are personal stories from my life experience, and LCJP (Longmont Community Justice Partnership) stories based on actual experiences in restorative justice Circles, with name changes and enough content disguise to protect participants' privacy. Some stories are composites of various Circles that capture common experiences of restorative justice. Some LCJP stories are retold by me and others come from Linda Leary, a writer who volunteers with our program and helps us capture some of the cases in writing. Some stories are multicultural teaching tales that are retold by Lana Leonard, my partner in founding Teaching Peace. Stories appear in italics set apart in a block and are interspersed throughout the book to illustrate and emphasize various points. I also included quotes from actual apology letters that are reprinted as written, with no corrections of spelling or grammar, except that identifying information has been altered to protect privacy.

This book is also an homage to the hundreds of Circle members I've sat among who showed up with the moral courage to listen and tell their truth. I have tried to recount their stories with fidelity while not breeching any privacy agreements. I often sat in these Circles with the awareness that though I was in the facilitator chair, in truth, at some point in my life I could be in any seat in the Circle. I hope their stories will serve to strengthen the common bonds of our humanity and enlarge our compassionate hearts.

Beverly Title
Longmont, Colorado
June 2011

Chapter 1
The Ancients

If there is not one among us who contains sufficient wisdom, many people together may find a clear path.
Paula Underwood Spencer — Turtle Woman Singing
from *The Walking People*

It was not the first time Young Hunter had taken more than seemed his fair share of the meat, but Man Hunter felt anger as Young Hunter, this time, took the pelt as well. True, he had stalked the prey and fired the first arrow that stopped it cold. But now there were more mouths to feed in Man Hunter's lodge, and he needed to bring home enough food. He was sure Young Hunter was greedy, his chest filled with pride, concerned with showing off his bounty. As they neared the village, all could see there was ill will, each hunter grabbing, arguing. It was clear from the way they carried their bodies and the force of their feet meeting the ground. As Others neared, they began to take sides.

An Elder stood apart, watching as the people became caught up in the squabble. He held his staff straight into the air and gave a mighty ululating cry that sounded above the din. All heads turned and saw their leader bidding them to Central Fire. Heads flung back defiantly, the hunters came toward the center of the camp. They sat on opposite sides of the fire, each with family and friends nearby. They found familiar places and sat in a Circle around the warm heart of their community.

After a time of silence, the Elder began to chant a familiar prayer, asking for help in finding a path to harmony among the people. The people began to soften and became humble as they realized they had gotten caught up in pettiness; deep down inside they knew they would all suffer, perhaps perish, if their hunters fought among themselves, if the people failed to respect each other's need. If either hunter were banished, his survival alone would be unlikely. The gravity of the situation hung in the air like a heavy fog.

The Elder spoke to them. "In this Circle, all voices will be heard," he said. "Everyone will be respected equally. We will pass the talking stick so each may speak fully without interruption. Only Truth may be spoken and from understanding each other, together we will find our way..."

It likely came about something like this. Conflict over the hunt or a potential mate, the very things that clog our courts today, threatened the well-being of the people. And there were elders who had seen such events divide and destroy once strong clans. Everyone understood exile from the tribe was tantamount to a death sentence. Some wise elder probably first recognized the possibility of a better strategy than a bonk on the head and might makes right. Somewhere, some time the first win-win scenario was conceived, as powerful as was the conception of the zero in mathematics.

This is probably how conflict resolution strategies were first devised and tested, then refined and used successfully for millennia. Then these ancient methods of speaking and listening were co-opted by courts and kings of conquering people, those who figured out how to profit from others' discord, and they were lost to society — until recently.

Today the ancient teachings are being given back to us. Shamans from around the globe are honoring ancient prophesy by sharing their teachings with their non-Native brothers and sisters. The condor of South America is soaring with our eagle of North America in the hope that, together, these mighty birds may be able to guide us away from a path of destruction. Indigenous people, those who "never forgot to remember" as Paula Underwood so dearly called them in *The Walking People*, [2] are now teaching us these ancient methods that just might save our modern selves:

"YOU HAVE SEEN HOW IT IS
That we are an Enduring People –
    One who continues in the Chosen Purpose
    Against great difficulties.

"YET YOU HAVE SEEN HOW IT IS"
    —and she traced in the air
    the closing of the circle of her thoughts—

    "that we are a Young People —
        like small ones
            whose teachers go away
                before they have learned enough
who quarrel
    over the resolution of this and that.

"SO
    LET US NOW LEARN HOW TO BE A PEOPLE
        WHO SEEK THE WISDOM OF ORDERED
        COUNCIL.

"LET US REMEMBER
    HOW QUICKLY ONE WHO LEADS
        MAY BE TAKEN FROM US.

"LET US UNDERSTAND
    THAT WHAT IS IMPOSSIBLE FOR ONE

MAY BE POSSIBLE FOR MANY.
"AND IF ALL THIS ESCAPES YOUR MEMORY
REMEMBER ONLY THIS:
  SEEK THE WISDOM OF ORDERED COUNCIL—

"HOWEVER MANY
  HOWEVER FEW
    HOWEVER OLD
      HOWEVER YOUNG

"SEEK THE WISDOM OF ORDERED COUNCIL.

"Let even the youngest among you
  sit and be heard."

Today a movement called restorative justice is gathering momentum around the world. It is informed by the wisdom and generosity of the Maori of New Zealand, various African tribal traditions, Native American Peacemakers, the First People of Canada and indigenous people of every continent.

My gratitude is great for the ancient ones . . .

- Who had the clarity to appreciate the essential value of *every* person;

- Who recognized the possibility of solutions that satisfied all, based in something more than superior force;

- Who understood the integral wisdom of a Circle for telling our stories and finding solutions together;

- Who envisioned the eventual need of a conquering people to also risk extinction without a justice that preserves dignity and rebuilds relationships;

- Who lived in harmony with the earth and inherently knew how to respect all creation;

- Who loved Earth and all her creatures enough to share their justice despite past injustice to them;

- Who dedicated their lives to carrying the oral traditions and bringing the stories to us now;

- Who foresaw our inevitable spiritual evolution to be a People Who Can Listen And Learn;

- Who shared their knowing with us that there might be a bridge from their ancient wisdom to our modern times where it is so clearly needed.

Chapter 2
The Moderns

With the dramatic, often violent, changes occurring at this time in history, it is important for all of us to learn how to best use our talents for a better and more peaceful world.

—President Jimmy Carter

As the turn of the millennium drew near, there was a town in the north end of Boulder County, Colorado, where something magical happened. In 1996 a group of people came together, a band of peacemakers, whose arrogance had been stripped away by the stark light of a community, not unlike others, whose children were forming gangs and committing acts of violence. There was a police chief who was bold enough to expose the Emperor's wardrobe problem by publicly declaring that the criminal justice system was broken. He saw that the current systems were not solving the problems and became a mighty spokesman for this other way, the restorative way, that was emerging.

The bold citizens knew that something had to be done. They came together to be a part of the solution, and that solution was called Restorative Justice (RJ). They had heard of the indigenous ways of addressing criminal wrongdoing that emphasized respect for all people and establishing right relationships, that put the problem in the hands of the people most directly involved and reduced dependence on "the system." They intuitively grasped the efficacy of the restorative circle process. The inner knowing and instant recognition of the rightness of restorative justice was so strong, it was as if their DNA still held an imprint of this ancient way.

This resolute group was made up of committed citizens, retired scientists, educators, women who worked in hardware stores, counselors, massage therapists, storytellers, mothers and fathers, grandparents, all with this in common; they held a rock-solid belief in the inherent worth of all people, and they were fearless.

Inspired by the belief in a better way and guided by the indigenous wisdom of the Maori of New Zealand, they formed a partnership of police, courts, schools and nonprofits and, together, they grew arms long and strong enough to gather to them the youth of this community who were committing criminal acts and engaging in violence. They were certain that the young ones needed to be held closer, listened to more deeply and valued more fully, as they didn't understand that they were an important part of a larger whole called Community. The young ones did not yet understand that when you hurt another, you are hurting yourself, and those you love as well. The peacemakers knew that all this had to be done with firm accountability for harmful behavior, and, if it were to succeed, the accountability had to come in a context of care that the young ones could feel.

"In the restorative justice circle I learned what community is. It has always been some vague term that had no real meaning for me. But here I saw real people, people who cared about me. People gave up their time to sit here and help me figure out what I needed to do to fix this mess I had made. They didn't judge me. They didn't make me feel like a loser, which is what I expected. They just cared about me and wanted to help me. They made me feel like I wanted to be a part of this community thing."

– A teen offender from the Longmont Community Justice Partnership

My Introduction to Restorative Justice

I had spent 21 years as a public school educator, creating alternative schools for students who were marginalized and withering in the traditional system. During that time I had completed a Ph.D. with an emphasis in conflict resolution, implemented peer mediation and conflict resolution in 14 schools, and developed one of the first national programs for bullying prevention. When I met Lana, I was exhausted.

Lana was a multicultural storyteller who thrilled me with tales of ancient wisdom, "tales that teach without preaching," she would say. I loved that idea! From first meeting we recognized a sister's bond, and we soon discovered we had been born within hours of each other. She had heard of my work for some time and knew it was closely aligned with her own. She knew she wanted to make a contribution to the greater good with her life, and she decided the most important thing she could do, she later told me, was to support my work. Together we dreamed aloud of founding a nonprofit dedicated to peacemaking.

"But, Lana," I said, "I'm just too tired. I do not think I have enough juice to do it." "Don't worry," was her reply, "I'll carry you." In 1994 we founded Teaching Peace with this mission: To cultivate attitudes, skills and opportunities for living peacefully with self, others and the world.

Thom Allena, a consultant I met at a conference, first told me about restorative justice, and the concept instantly resonated. When he said he was a consultant in that field, I told him I had no idea what restorative justice was, but I was sure it was important, so I wrote those two words on my note pad— restorative justice.

Months later, Lana and I were at another conference where we met some people who were actually practicing restorative justice. I had been working in partnership with the police and youth-serving agencies through my years in the school district, and I thought our community was ripe for such a project. We had a visionary police

15

chief and city leaders and innovative school leaders. I told Lana I felt compelled to follow this, and she agreed. Thom said he would help, and he brought Mark Seidler, his friend and colleague; their expertise as consultants and trainers proved critical to our early success.

With the help of our police chief, we received a grant and formed the Longmont Community Justice Partnership (LCJP) with the police, the municipal court, the school district and a nonprofit that worked with at-risk youth.

With the help of our police chief, we received a grant and formed the Longmont Community Justice Partnership (LCJP) with the police, the municipal court, the school district and a nonprofit that worked with at-risk youth. Teaching Peace became the managing partner, and as executive director of Teaching Peace, I also became the program director of LCJP. Lana was our first conference coordinator.

This is where that team of peacemakers, introduced at the start of this chapter, entered the scene. Each of the partner agencies committed to finding at least one person who would volunteer to be trained and facilitate justice Circles. It was not long before restorative justice was the hottest new ticket in town, and we had volunteers showing up from neighboring towns as well as our own. These folks were innovators, and they ran on the passion of a great cause combined with this deeply appealing and inherently wise process.

∞§∞

The Life Cycle of an LCJP Case

There will be much more about restorative justice in subsequent chapters. For now, here is an overview of the process used at the

Longmont Community Justice Partnership (LCJP). In other communities, RJ programs are structured differently. As long as there is fidelity to the principles and values of restorative justice, the forms may vary. It should also be noted that facilitators have their own styles; the exact ways they conduct Circles also vary. Here is a brief explanation of a typical Circle process at the LCJP, though much of it applies broadly to RJ programs. The italicized text following each section tells the story of a LCJP case told in serial style, each installment illustrating the content of that section.

The Referral - When a police officer refers a case to restorative justice, the office staff reads the police report and then makes telephone contact with the primary parties (victim and family, offender and family) to explain the process and make sure they want to participate. The staff determines if the offender is taking responsibility for the crime. Restorative justice does not use an evidentiary process to determine guilt or innocence; the ticket to get in the RJ door is the offender taking responsibility for his behavior. RJ is a voluntary process for everyone. In rare circumstances, a victim may decide not to participate, usually because they are "over it" or too embarrassed, *etc.* In those cases, if the victim agrees, we may decide to proceed using a surrogate victim to represent the victim's harm. If not, which rarely happens, the case is given back to one of our Liaison Officers. (More on the Liaison Officers later in this chapter.)

LCJP received a referral from a school resource officer of a sexual harassment case. A middle school girl had been repeatedly harassed about her "developing figure" by three boys at school. When the LCJP office staff made contact, the young girl was mortified of the topic and refused to participate in restorative justice. Her mother was adamant that these boys be held accountable for their behavior, so the staff decided to assign it to a team of facilitators to

17

preconference with this girl and her mother to see if they could arrive at a solution. Perhaps the girl would change her mind, as sometimes happens, or perhaps a surrogate victim could speak for her.

The Preconference - If the offender accepts responsibility and the parties agree to participate, the case is given to a facilitator and a cofacilitator. This pair of facilitators, who are trained community volunteers, makes contact with the parties again and conducts what we call a preconference which is usually held in the primary parties' homes. The preconference is an opportunity to hear everyone's stories, prepare them for what the Circle process will be like, what they will need to talk about, and answer any of their questions. The facilitators are determining if it is reasonable to believe the case can safely come to Circle and not do further harm. Community members are selected based on their ability to represent the harm of this crime to the community, and their capacity to be respectful and compassionate to all parties. Preconferencing for community members and additional participants, like school personnel and police officers, is usually done by telephone.

For the preconference, the team of two facilitators went to the home of this girl and her mother. It was quickly apparent that a face-to-face meeting of this nature between the girl and these boys would add further trauma and revictimize her. After the facilitators were clear that it was not safe for the girl to participate, they explored the option of having a surrogate victim represent her in the Circle. Her mother agreed to take on that role, and, upon considering the advantages, the girl concurred. After answering questions and explaining the process, the facilitators went to the boys' homes. There they met with the boys and their parents, laid out the process, answered questions and heard each boy's story.

18

The Circle - At this point, the facilitator determines to call the Circle that may be held in a community room at the Safety and Justice Building, at the Teaching Peace headquarters in an old Victorian home, in a school, or at another community site. At the designated time and place, the Circle assembles. As people enter the room they see a circle of chairs with nametags to designate their seats. There is no table, and everyone is in full sight of each other. The Circle is typically composed of the victim[*] and his or her chosen support people, almost always family members; the offender with chosen support people, typically family members; two or three adult and teen community members, a police officer, other professionals, such as counselors or probation officers, as relevant to the specific Circle, a facilitator and a cofacilitator. If the offender is a teen, we always try to have at least one teen community member in the Circle. The victim and offender groups are typically seated on either side of the facilitator, and the cofacilitator is directly across the Circle from the facilitator, nearest the door.

The facilitator begins by welcoming everyone and asking all to introduce themselves with their name and their relationship to this Circle.

I'm Mary's mother and I'm here to speak on her behalf today . . . I'm John and I said things to Mary . . .I'm Tom, John's father. . . I'm Terry . . . I'm a counselor at the middle school. . . . I'm Officer Chris, the school resource officer at the middle school.

---

[*] Terms victim and offender are used here to designate roles. In a Circle, these persons are addressed by their names, and the labels would not be used.

19

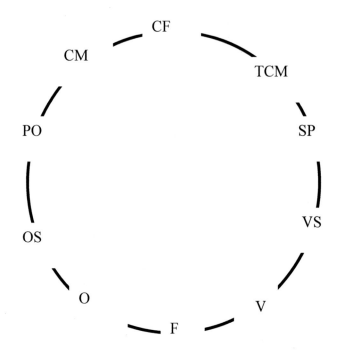

F	Facilitator	CM	Community Member
CF	Cofacilitator	*TCM	Teen Community
V	Victim		Member
VS	Victim Support	*SP	School Personnel
O	Offender	*PO	Police Officer
OS	Offender Support		

* Optional roles as appropriate to the Circle

Diagram 1. Seating Arrangement of a Typical Restorative Justice Circle

The facilitator states the purpose of the circle, establishes ground rules about respectful participation, truth telling, only speaking when it is your turn and protecting people's privacy. After all agree to the guidelines, the offender is asked to begin by telling his story of what happened. What he did and why he did it. What he was thinking about at the time. Who was affected and how?

"We were just goofing around, and I guess Mary was affected," *says John. The facilitator interrupts, "John, the goofing around* *part sounds like an excuse. I'd like you to start again and tell us* *what you did, what you were thinking and who was affected."* *He tries again and, with his head down, tells what he did. Then* *the other two boys speak of their contributions to the* *harassment.*

There are often tears as the story is being told, and the offender's mother is usually the first person to cry. Once the story is told, the Circle may ask any clarifying questions, not interrogations, to be sure all the facts are clear. At this point the offenders' parents often spontaneously apologize to the victim.

Next, it is the victim's turn to speak, and the facilitator asks her to focus on how she was affected by what happened, what harm was done and what she thinks should happen to repair that harm.

"My daughter used to jump out of bed in the morning eager to *go to school. Now I have to nag and push to get her out the* *door. When I ask about the changes, she tells me that kids at* *school don't like her and make fun of her. She says she wants* *to just stop growing up, because the boys all make fun of her,* *and it's so embarrassing; she just wants to hide in the* *bathroom. Her grades have dropped significantly, and she* *doesn't even want to go out of the house."* *Mom starts to* *choke up and tears come. "Do you boys remember what it* *was like to have your voice crack? Growing up and having*

21

your body change is hard. I want you boys to find something better to do with your time than harassing young women, and just cut it out!"

Support people, community members, police and other participants tell of the harm from their points of view, while the cofacilitator keeps notes of the harms and repair items as those are stated. After the harms have all been surfaced, the offender is asked to recap the harm. He is given an opportunity to address the Circle, and this opening typically elicits a series of soulful, sobbing apologies. If he can do a reasonably thorough job of recounting the harms done, the rest of the process tends to go smoothly.

At this point the Circle takes a dramatic turn to focus on the assets of the offender. LCJP developed an Assets Survey that was informed by *What Kids Need to Succeed*[3] by Peter Benson of the Search Institute. The offender and the facilitators or LCJP office staff complete this questionnaire prior to the Circle, and the cofacilitator reviews some of the highlights with the Circle.

Tom, Mark and Luis are all on the football team. They are athletes and all three of them have pretty good grades. Tom is good at math; Mark has strong mechanical talents; Luis is artistically gifted. Mark has younger siblings he babysits, and he's really good at playing with younger kids. All three boys are considered to be leaders in the school.

Numerous offenders have reported after the Circle that the review of their assets was the turning point for them. When they heard their strengths being reported, it felt like restorative justice was "for real." After a Circle one offender asked her facilitator if she could have her assets page, because she wanted to put it up on the wall in her room. Respect for victim's feelings requires that we prepare them in advance of the Circle for the Assets Phase and to explain its importance in preventing future victimization.

Next, ideas are generated for how to repair harm. Though some ideas have already come out, the facilitator directs the Circle to brainstorm and come up with as many ideas as possible for how this offender may use his strengths, his assets to repair the harm to the victim, to the community, to himself and his family. They are instructed that the Agreement will have three to five items, and each item must be measurable (we have to know when it is completed); it has to be achievable (within the offender's capacity); and it has to be relevant (must fit the crime, cannot be generic.) Repair of harm to the offender is framed in terms of what will help him make better future choices. The facilitators do not give ideas to the Circle; their job is to conduct the process and leave the content up to the Circle. The cofacilitator is asked to review the ideas. Then a crucial moment in the Circle occurs when the offender is asked to self-sentence. The facilitator turns to the offender and says, "Having heard all this, what will you do to make things right?"

> *"We need to write apology letters to Mary, and we need to be respectful of her. We can also work with the counselor on the idea she put out in the Circle about starting a respect program at school. We also need to do some work at home for our parents to pay back the time they've had to spend dealing with this mess."* The facilitator suggests that being respectful of Mary may be hard to measure, and asks the boys if they are willing to make a Good Faith Agreement about that. They say they are, so she asks each boy to state his intention around respect for Mary to Mary's mother and make her a promise in front of everyone here. They do. She asks how many hours will need to be given to help the counselor and for helping out their parents. Each item is checked that it is measurable, achievable and relevant to the offense.

After the offender chooses the items for his Agreement, the victim and then everyone else is asked if this would satisfy them.

23

The question is then asked, "If he does those things, will the Circle be willing to recognize him as being honorable and responsible for his behavior and taking direct action to repair the harm? Will it satisfy you?" If anyone does not agree, the facilitator negotiates with the offender around what that person needs until all agree. A date is set by which all items must be completed or the case will be referred back to the police for processing. The Circle participants are congratulated and instructed to sign the Agreement and complete a feedback form before leaving. They are invited to enjoy some refreshments, sometimes called Breaking Bread, while the cofacilitator writes up the Agreement. During this informal time together, it is common to witness hugs, handshakes, and congratulations, even sharing of contact information.

> *Mary's mom represented her brilliantly in the Circle, and the boys demonstrated more and more remorse as the Circle proceeded. Each boy looked embarrassed, and it was hard, at first, to own their behavior fully. By the end, their affect had brightened. During Breaking Bread, the father of one of the boys thanked Mary's mother for helping his son figure out how to fix this. He hated to think that Mary had been so badly affected. Before the Circle, he said, his son thought it was kind of a compliment to Mary; now he understands that he crossed the line, and his father doesn't think his son will do that again. The Circle had done its work well, and, in that moment, I believed this father was right.*

Monitoring - The LCJP office staff monitors the agreement to completion or to the due date and notifies the victim and the referring agency of whether or not the offender completed the Agreement.

In this case, all three boys completed their agreements.

∞§∞

Here's an account of a Circle from a Community Member's perspective:

Shattered Trust and a Second Chance
As told by Linda Leary

We sat quietly in the silence taking measure of each other. The facilitator had made the introductions and laid out the rules for the conference. Emotions may run high, we will respect another's speaking without interruption, we will not accuse or be profane to another, we would share our truths as we saw it and we will honor the confidentiality of this proceeding. In this conference we were to listen to and participate in the restorative process of a young woman of 18 who is a substance abuser and instigator in check fraud. I don't think our young offender had much of an idea about Restorative Justice, except that it held the possibility of no jail time if the process went well. She sat composed, a forced smile on her face, with little idea of what was to come.

The conference began with our young offender telling her story. She was presently in drug rehab in another state and halfway through a six-month program. She described all the harm that was done from her present perspective. It was apparent early on that she did not see far past the personal harm let alone what had happened within her own family. She knew there was damage, but not until the conference moved forward with all members having their say was she finally overcome with the impact of how far reaching was her singular act.

My determination to stay cool and aloof fell by the wayside as her parents shared with obvious pain their experience of the last year.

25

Embarrassment, suppressed anger and shame rose to the surface as they described the events that nearly tore apart a marriage and ruptured a family unit into irreparable pieces. I could sense their helplessness and exhaustion. Who was this person that was once their perfect little girl? What caused her to go from honor student to addict who stole from her family and friends?

The conference heated up. Officer Jarvis (name changed for this piece) spoke. Dressed in jeans, tee shirt and sneakers, his uniform of the day, he worked in the offender's school among the students on a daily basis. "His kids" he called them and he knew our young woman personally. He expressed honestly his sadness and disappointment when he had to arrest one of his own. He felt responsible that he could not help her and where was the trust?

The victim here was a bank where the checks were written. A young bank officer came and shared with all of us what it costs banks annually in check fraud. Over $830 million per year! I nearly gasped. Most of these are written on accounts of hard working folks who scrape and save to put a few dollars together. Some of their accounts are wiped out overnight not to mention the destruction of their credit rating. Our young offender popped her eyes wide in new realization. So did I.

We were knee deep in it now. We all leaned into the circle. These could be my neighbors or my family and we as a 'family' had a problem. I had never met them before today, but we were no longer strangers; too much was on the table and we all felt it. We needed to work together to get through this.

As representatives of the community at large, my job plus that of my counterpart was to listen to all the input and then share from our perspective how we saw potential harm to the community from the offense committed by our young woman. Since we had no personal involvement with the offender or the victim, we came to the circle with "new eyes." From this vantage point we could observe and listen and often noted things that may have been missed in the comments of the others. We spoke from our hearts our own truths about the ripple effect of this crime. I spoke as if we were related, part of the same community family; and in this moment I believed it.

She Who Could Have Been My Daughter lost her composure. The apologies she had been giving throughout the conference up to this point had been only words, believed perhaps, but not entirely felt at the core of her being. This time she could barely speak the words as she turned first to her parents and said the words she had probably said many times before, "I am so sorry." "I don't know what to do to make you trust me again." I do not know how to explain the shift that occurred but we all felt it as something real and palpable. Not one of us was left unmoved. For the first time we felt hope; and we ALL wanted to move forward to begin the restorative, healing process of this damaged little community. There had been no shame or blame placed on one person in this conference. We addressed behavior and actions and the harm and consequences of those actions. We addressed the strong points of this young woman and her potential and ability to affect a whole community in a positive way if she so chose it.

Finally, we brainstormed for ideas that would lead to agreements and a measurable plan that would repair the harm and allow possibility for healing of all parties involved. Once consensus was reached and all agreed, a contract was drawn and signed by everyone present. I felt like I was signing a document as important as the Constitution. Not one of us in the room took this process lightly. Once again the offender had choice in the matter. She knew that by signing and completing all the agreements as stated, she had the opportunity to resolve the criminal case and recreate herself as a functioning community member with dignity. If she broke even one agreement, the contract would be considered null and void and her case would go back into the mainline justice system.

We completed the conference and opened the circle. We shared food and talked to one another. I hugged the young woman and congratulated her on her courage to participate. Her mother came up and hugged me and thanked me for my input and support. My eyes misted over. Where only two hours before we were constrained and aloof, we were now a community of people who had counseled together and created something profound.

Restoration had begun. There was much more to do; but now there was an opening for possibility where before there was none. When we give up having to be right and to punish but focus instead on the good of the whole, miracles occur. The simple act of listening, really listening to each other, is magic. And therein lies a huge difference.

∞§∞

But Does It Work?

Some people characterize restorative justice as soft. But offenders do not. Many report it being much more rigorous to face those you have harmed and hear their stories than to let an attorney speak for you to a judge. And many victims appreciate having the opportunity to face those who harmed them and to tell their story fully, not just answer the questions the attorneys choose to ask. Police appreciate having a say in how harm is repaired. Community members are deeply satisfied to contribute to safety and well being by showing an offender what

> **90% of the offenders completed their Circle Agreements**

harm has rippled out from his behavior and what importance his life has to their community.

Most people hearing about restorative justice think it sounds really good, but they always want to know if it really works. By this they mean, what do the numbers say. What kinds of outcomes do you get; how does this method measure up?

Teaching Peace contracted with an independent research firm to build a database to capture the information we would need to answer those questions. We knew we would need funding to do our work, and as soon as the funders heard the stories, the qualitative data, they would want the numbers, the quantitative data. To help secure the best possible, most reliable outcome data for the funders and to help us analyze and refine our processes, we had our data periodically analyzed by the National Research Center, an independent evaluation firm. The report they provided was a collective analysis of data sets from 2001-2002, 2003-2004, and 2005-2006. They looked for trends to determine if the outstanding results we saw early on were just a flash in the pan, or if the outcomes held up over time.

What they concluded was that 90% of the offenders completed their Circle Agreements. Of those who completed, only 10% were rearrested by the Longmont Police within a one-year period, the most likely time frame for recidivism or reoffending. People always ask me how this compares to the traditional justice system that has recidivism rates of 70% or higher. Boulder County is proud of its 50% recidivism rate, as well it should be. Though we cannot help but care about such things as a frame of reference, it is really an apples to oranges comparison, as the criminal justice system does not have the luxury of only taking cases where offenders plead guilty.

In restorative justice we are adamant about saying that we are not just offender-focused, but we serve three clients: the victim, the offender and the community. To measure our success in that arena, we use a self-report questionnaire for Circle participants to let us know about their experience of RJ. Was it fair; was it just; did it meet their needs? Our results consistently show that 95% or better of *all* participant groups were satisfied or highly satisfied with their experience of restorative justice. I think these are the most telling numbers of all and are perhaps fairly compared to the traditional justice system where satisfaction rates may be as low as 10%.

So, to answer the question: "Does restorative justice work?" Some say that the empirical data from experimental design research are insufficient to make that claim. More and more, it is being recognized as an Evidence-Based Practice, which means there are sufficient scientific data to support its effectiveness. Admittedly, restorative justice does not work in every case, and it is not appropriate for every case. However, there is a mounting body of evidence to suggest that restorative justice is an extremely valuable addition to our justice toolbox. I have attended three international RJ conferences and heard reports from program people doing RJ throughout the world. The outcome data reported are amazingly consistent; across cultures and geography, the RJ outcomes show that it works about 90% of the time with high satisfaction rating from participants.

The full report, *The Longmont Community Justice Partnership: a report of findings*, is available at www.lcjp.org/learn-more. The concluding statement of the Executive Summary of this report says, "LCJP is to be commended for its record of performance."

> **Our results consistently show that 95% or better of *all* participant groups were satisfied or highly satisfied with their experience of restorative justice.**

Many additional RJ evaluation reports can be found at the International Institute of Restorative Practices. See their website www.iirp.org, and click on Library.

∞§∞

It Takes a Village

After one facilitator meeting, I told Lana that I felt like I was holding the reins on a team of stallions, and it took all I could do to steer them in the same direction. There were 3 wise elders – Richard, Al, and Meir – who brought experience in business, in psychotherapy, in sustainability and wordsmithing. Meir produced a *Lexicon of Restorative Justice* and led us as we struggled against the language of the criminal justice system, such as "offender" and "victim." Anne, another member of this talented team, came with an extensive background in working with crime victims and a great gift for knowing how to get things done. Sarah, Kathee, Carol, Gary, Bea contributed to meeting after meeting, all smart, good-hearted, and fully present, and Katie, who was later elected to our City Council, arrived at meetings with freshly baked cookies. There was rampant enthusiasm and eagerness that initiated this project.

Over the years, new waves of volunteers have shown up, probably thousands by now, some with professional backgrounds, many without. Will and Walt, Jessica, Connie and Maciel, Kappy and Kris, and Kevin, Leslie and Meg and Susan, Roberta, Bertrand, Gary, Marian and Linda Lu, Dan, Lauren, Rogelio, Greg, Diana and Deb and Opalanga to name but a few. I include these names here, though only a fraction of them, to impart that these were real people, and there were many of them who were bold enough and with sufficient moral courage to facilitate restorative justice circles in the early days when we were eager but lacking experience. And there were those who supported us in other significant ways, like David, my honeyman, who fed our bodies and our souls with his magnificent cooking and loving heart – ever steady. The roots of volunteerism have grown strong in our organization, and they still sustain this work today.

Roger, an air traffic consultant, mows the lawn, which really helps us look good. Jan, a people charmer, shows up to serve food and drinks at events. Linda, a writer, interviews participants and facilitators and captures their stories. Many bright tech-savvy folks contribute IT support. Others make financial contributions, consistently responding to our fundraising campaigns, like "$101 for a 101 Ways to Peace."

Police officers volunteer to be Liaison Officers and support the use of restorative processes within their department. Having liaison officers has been a big boost to our success within the police department. They sit in Circles when requested if the arresting officer is unavailable. Additionally, the police liaisons agree to take any cases that are referred back to the police from LCJP, because the involved parties were unwilling to participate, or when agreements are not completed. They, then, do the follow up required to resolve the case; most often the offender is issued a ticket or court summons.

My daughter, Summer, stepped up for four years and brought extraordinary leadership, shored up the organizational structures and enhanced efficiencies at Teaching Peace. How wonderful for me to have the opportunity to do this most precious work of my heart with my only child, a daughter who brought her many gifts to the work. She had previously started a restorative justice program at the Boulder County Sheriff's Office, so she was knowledgeable about restorative justice and about partnering with a policing organization. Teaching Peace became much stronger with her in the mix.

This is why we have "community" and "partnership" in our name: the Longmont Community Justice Partnership. We truly are a partnership on many levels, with our governmental entities of police, courts and schools; with our nonprofit community of Alternatives for Youth and Teaching Peace. And the partnership extends to our wider community through the numerous members who reside in our area and take an active role in our organization. It makes me proud to live in a place where so many folks give their time, talent and resources in the name of "justice for all."

∞§∞

Lessons Well Learned

This visionary team continued to learn and grow, refining our processes at every step. We sat in hundreds of circles, learning with every one, expanding our heads and our hearts. We prebriefed and debriefed and, together, figured out how to adapt these ancient methods to a 21st century American community. We devised ways to take processes that had operated within intact communities where everyone knew each other from birth to death, and adapt them for Circles of multicultural, multilingual gatherings of people who may not have even met before. We learned to conduct civil proceedings that could include people of any or no religious affiliation and to make them sacred without the use of prayer or theological trappings.

Being a part of this amazing work for 15 years has been a gift that has taught me much that I share with you through this book. As our society has become more and more diverse and many people have moved away from traditional religions, we are in need of a social code that can lead us toward harmony with ourselves and with each

> **Relationship, Respect, Responsibility, Repair, and Reintegration teach us how to live together well and what to do to restore harmony when needed.**

other. The principles and values of RJ as summed up in the 5 R's of restorative justice provide such a guide. Relationship, Respect, Responsibility, Repair, and Reintegration teach us how to live together well and what to do to restore harmony when needed.

∞§∞

The Work Changes Us

LCJP started as an alternative sentencing program, a diversion to keep youth out of the criminal justice system. As we began to live by the principles and values of restorative justice, the 5 R's, they became guideposts for how we conducted ourselves. And then we noticed that there was a language imbedded in these values and principles and that that language had become infused in the way we spoke to others. By doing justice "for others," we found our own lives improved.

Educators and parents in our group spoke of how they were using the language with their kids and how effective it was. We came to know others who were applying the restorative principles and processes in school communities and calling it Restorative Discipline. We learned of social workers who were using the restorative approach in child welfare cases and calling it Family Group Decision Making. The term Restorative Practices emerged as an umbrella term to refer to all the various applications of these indigenous-inspired ways of addressing social issues based on a set of principles and values.

I began to pay closer and closer attention to the language that was inherent in all of these approaches, and a conflict resolution process based on the 5 R's took shape. RJ is not a program; it is a set of principles and values. This means it can be applied anywhere, not just in a formal Circle. RJ's emphasis on healing relationships makes it particularly valuable for navigating today's challenges.

One afternoon my husband and I were squabbling about something that I cannot even recall, when my daughter broke in. "Mom," she said, "Just listen to him tell you how he's been bothered by this situation." My daughter, also a restorative justice practitioner, shifted the whole tenor of the conversation with this one suggestion. As I remembered to listen to how he

34

was affected, I began to ask questions that made him feel heard instead of defending or justifying my own behavior. What needed to happen next soon became clear.

∞§∞

And The Work Goes On

One of the greatest testaments to the success of LCJP is that it continues. Today Teaching Peace has successfully navigated its founders' succession, and the work goes on. The next generation of leaders are really good people, just like you, doing the work of their hearts, strengthening our community and making a big difference in the lives of many.

Throughout this time Mike, the enlightened police chief, unafraid to say that the criminal justice system was broken, led a community policing initiative that became rated one of the top ten in the country. He has since been promoted to Director of Public Safety and now heads up both police and fire departments. He continues to serve on the Teaching Peace Board of Directors. Lana and her husband retired and moved to Sedona, Arizona, where she founded the Sedona Oak Creek Restorative Justice program. Some things are just too valuable to leave behind when you move. Mike and Lana continue to bring more models of excellence to the world. Lana retells this story that is purported to be true.

Turtles All the Way Down
Retold by Lana Leonard

William James, author of The Varieties of Religious Experience, *was giving a lecture on creation stories to an erudite crowd of theologians. There was an elder Indian woman*

35

in the back of the room who was listening intently to the creation stories from Genesis to stories from all over the world. At the end she quietly stopped Mr. James and said, "That was all very interesting, Mr. James, but all those stories are wrong."

He politely asked her what, then, was the "real" story. She replied that once the world was all water and turtle was the only one who was able to dive to the bottom and grab some dirt under her nails. She dove down again and again until she had enough mud to carry on her back, which eventually became Earth. To this day the world is called "Turtle Island". Mr. James said, "Excuse me, but what is holding up the turtle?" "Another turtle" she answered, as if he were ignorant indeed. "I'm so sorry to ask this again," said James, "but what is holding up that turtle?" She flatly declared to him, "Why, Mr. James, IT'S TURTLES ALL THE WAY DOWN!"

And so it is with Teaching Peace. Turtle, upon turtle, upon turtle, we hold each other up and bring new Earth to our community.

My gratitude is great for the modern ones . . .

- Who answer the call and show up;

- Who tenaciously wrestle every detail in developing and refining our practice;

- Who believe in the significance of every member of our community;

- Who show our youth the true meaning of Community;

- Who have the moral courage to create the safe container and hold the Circle;

- Who bear witness to others' pain and guide the Circle as it transmutes the heartache;

- Who walk a new spiritual path through our practice of restorative justice;

- Who never give up on our mission.

And additional thanks to all the communities everywhere who are embracing the restorative way and making our world a kinder, more compassionate and safer place for ourselves, for our children, and for our children's children. May we never again "forget to remember."

Chapter 3
Relationship – The First R

The meeting of two personalities is like the contact of two chemical substances; if there is any reaction, both are transformed.

—Carl Jung

Our practice of restorative justice at LCJP rests upon the 5 R's: Relationship, Respect, Responsibility, Repair and Reintegration. Each of the 5 R's has a chapter devoted exclusively to articulating the layers of meaning associated with it. Alternate chapters fill in the story of how these concepts are put into practice.

∞§∞

The Relationship Principle

Restorative justice recognizes that when a crime occurs, individuals and communities have been violated. It is the damage to these relationships that is primarily important and is the central focus of what restorative practices seek to address.

Where traditional justice focuses on the law that has been broken and frame that as an offense against the state, restorative justice focuses on how relationships have been affected and how people have been harmed. The emphasis is on individual harm and subsequent damage to relationships at the interpersonal and the community levels. Its primary emphasis on relationships is one important aspect that distinguishes RJ from related processes such as mediation. That is not to imply that processes like mediation do not focus on relationships, as they may, but restorative practices *always* do. Relationships are the primary focus of restorative practices. When relationships are strong, people experience more fulfilling lives and communities become places where we want to live.

> **Relationships are the primary focus of restorative practices. When relationships are strong, people experience more fulfilling lives and communities become places where we want to live.**

In his groundbreaking book, *Emotional Intelligence*[4], Harvard Professor Daniel Goleman posits that EQ (emotional intelligence) can be more important than IQ. He forwards the belief that the key to happiness lies in our ability to get along with others.

Sitting in hundreds of Circles has led me to believe that the ability to form, sustain and restore healthy relationships could well be the most important of all life skills. In fact, our ability to form strong, meaningful relationships with our family, friends, neighbors and coworkers may be the clearest measure of life success. The persons who do this well are most likely to have happy lives, regardless of any other measure of success they may or may not achieve, or hardships they must endure. Conversely, those who cannot or do not form strong bonds of attachment with others, regardless of any other achievements they may attain, are unlikely to find happiness.

> **Our ability to form strong, meaningful relationships with our family, friends, neighbors and coworkers may be the clearest measure of life success.**

40

The path to sustainable, positive relationships challenges us, and when we stumble on the inevitable potholes, we may retreat into the safety of our private spaces, both physical and emotional. Recently I told a friend that things were going really well with my husband and me, and I wanted to cherish this time, because it was sure to change. Relationships rarely progress in a straight line, but rather move forward in some kind of wave pattern that displays as small ups and downs or great crests of joy and sinking ebbs of disappointment or despair.

In our society we are quick to dispose of relationships if they get difficult. A divorce rate of 50% or higher is a clear indicator of this trend. Our tendency to incarcerate people for crimes, even though recidivism rates range from 50% to 70% or higher, is another indicator of our mistaken belief that we can simply dispose of our problem relationships. Neither solution, divorce nor imprisonment, has worked very well. Our children pay a heavy price for the divorce rate and for our prison systems, as we still spend more on prisons than schools. It actually costs more to incarcerate a juvenile than it does to send her to Harvard University! In 2009 the Justice Policy Institute reported the cost for incarcerating a juvenile at $241.99 a day, which equals $88,326 per year. That same year the Harvard University website lists *all* costs to attend, including tuition, books, room, board, travel, *etc.* at $58,006 per year. How can we ever hope to solve our budgetary, planetary and health care issues if we cannot live together more successfully and readjust our fear-based budget priorities?

Humans are clan animals, and it is our relationships with others that weave the social fabric of our society. Clearly some relationships are more important to us than others, but all relationships matter in some way. Life runs along more smoothly when even the fairly distant relationships, like with the checker at our local grocery, are harmonious, and we should never underestimate the value of a friendship; however, when our connection with our child or our brother or even our in-laws becomes challenging, it profoundly impacts our lives.

Relationships are the mechanism that supports our physical, mental and spiritual evolution as a species, and, ironically, it is the challenging relationships that have the most to teach us about ourselves and offer the greatest opportunity for our growth and personal development. What we do not like in others is almost always hiding in our own shadows. What pushes our buttons in someone else is a mirror to our own soul, and self-reflection about that trait holds the promise of personal insight.

Generally speaking, the greater our negative reaction, the greater the likelihood we have much to learn from it. In her book, *The Revolutionary Agreements*[5], Marian Head recommends that we make a personal agreement to "Look within when I react." If you find something annoying in someone else, sit quietly and ask yourself how that very thing shows up in you. In the privacy of our own heart and mind, we can discover a portal of insight that leads to new levels of compassion and acceptance for ourselves and others.

One of our facilitators told this story at a facilitator team meeting.

She was conducting a Circle for a 12 year-old who was having a lot of trouble admitting what he had done. The victim was adamant that the boy had, in fact, hit her and taken her backpack. He insisted he had only found the backpack and then returned it.

The facilitator was about to call off the Circle and send the case back to the police when she had an idea. She told everyone that restorative justice comes from the way ancient people worked out their problems. In ancient times they would call on the ancestors for help when they didn't know what to do. She instructed the Circle to take a few minutes of silence and think about their ancestors and what they would say about this situation. In only a few minutes the boy burst out, "My grandmother always told me that things would be better if I just told the truth. I did hit her and take the backpack, and I was just too scared to say so."

That told, the Circle did its work and came to a good Agreement.

When there are bumps in our relationships, it takes courage to confront the challenges and move beyond. It also requires commitment to sustain relationships through the hard times. When my husband and I were dating and hit our first big bump, I was ready to move on. It was he who said, "No, I'm not a bag of garbage you can just throw out. You said you were willing to be in this relationship, so sit down. We've got work to do." He was the first man to refuse my exit invitation. We recently celebrated our 30th year of marriage because of his wisdom about commitment and our mutual interest in honoring that commitment. Enduring relationships require commitment.

∞§∞

It helps to understand conflict as neither good nor bad. Conflict itself is value neutral, and it can be constructive or destructive, depending on how we manage it. Constructive conflicts help us to understand each other better and offer the promise of deeper appreciation and regard for each other. Destructive conflicts leave scars, and most of us have experienced enough of the latter

> **Conflict itself is value neutral, and it can be constructive or destructive, depending on how we manage it.**

to leave us averse to doing conflict at all. Avoiding conflict may be a good short-term strategy; however, is a destructive solution in the long term, especially if the relationship is significant.

In *Getting to Yes,*[6] authors Ronald Fisher and William Ury advocate being tough on the problem and soft on the people. This valuable resource on conflict is an important guide for doing conflict constructively. From a restorative perspective, it is important to remember that we can mend suffering relationships by being accountable for our actions and taking direct action to repair the harm. We will look more at how to do this in the Responsibility chapter.

> **From a restorative perspective, it is important to remember that we can mend suffering relationships by being accountable for our actions and taking direct action to repair the harm.**

Here is the story of how a young man, through his community service, found a powerful relationship in an unlikely place that brought wisdom to his life and satisfaction for his victims.

School was dismissed early, because heavy snow had been falling all day and showed no signs of stopping soon. A teen with his SUV full of friends was driving around town having fun by sliding his vehicle into snow banks, spraying slush on pedestrians. A couple walking their dog were among his victims. Other drivers who witnessed his behavior called the police. The young man took responsibility for the act, but insisted it "was just a prank." The pedestrians saw it very differently; they considered it an assault with a deadly weapon and were adamant that the youth do 100 hours of service to someone who had been seriously injured in an automobile accident. He was also to write a letter of apology to the pedestrians. He balked hard at the 100 hours, but conceded when the police officer in his Circle prepared to write a careless driving ticket that would cost him his license and have major impact on his insurance rates for years to come. A few days after Circle, we received this apology letter:

> Dear Mr. and Mrs. Angelo,
>
> I sincerely apologize for my driving. Getting you wet was accidental, due to poor road conditions. I feel terrible for causing such an inconvenience in your lives. Please accept my deepest apologies.
>
> Sincerely,
>
> Tom

Our staff determined the letter unacceptable and asked Tom to do his service and then write another letter. To avoid revictimization, we did not forward this letter to the victims. Several months later we received the second letter:

> Dear Mr. and Mrs. Angelo,
>
> I have completed all of the requirements of the agreement which was set by our group meeting. I have learned a lot from this program, and I support the whole idea. I believe that a ticket would not have had near as much of an affect on me. And I thank you for the decision you made [the victims' decision to allow the case to go to restorative justice.] The part of our plan that had the biggest affect was the 100 hours of volunteer work. I did these at ... a care center, which is a retirement home. I worked in the activities department; some of my duties included one-on-ones, leading group activities and assisting with physical therapy. During one-on-ones I would talk with the residents about anything and everything. For group activities I would help the residents make arts and crafts, serve food, and visit with them.

I did not spend too much time with the people in physical therapy, but I did spend countless hours with one certain resident during one-on–ones. His name was "Captain" Fred James and he had lost the use of his legs while working on a car with his son, it slipped off of the blocks and rolled over his legs. The incident had a major impact on his life and mine. If this poor man still had the use of his legs he would not have to be in this retirement home which he hated everything about. He was a very nice man but he was also very depressed. He told me all about his life from childhood to the car accident.

Seeing his sadness made me realize that by driving carelessly I could have caused a similar or even worse problem in your lives. I would not want to be responsible for something like that. I sincerely apologize for what I did to you, it was foolish, irresponsible, and stupid. Knowing what I know now in the same situation I would not have done it.

Sincerely,

Tom.

Tom went to college a few months after completing his agreement, and we heard that he continued to visit the Captain when he was back home.

The Power of Friendship

The next story illustrates the power of relationship, even from the grave. It comes from another restorative justice project we took on at a local high school that was suffering deeply from the explosive violence of two rival gangs of female students. Our staff person, also a former student of that school, met for two years in Circle with these girls before she found the opening that brought them together and changed everything.

Heart of Gangland

As told by Linda Leary

It was an election day, and people were lined up to vote at one of the local high schools. This school had a reputation for violence, creating fear among parents, teachers and students. Two female gangs operated within the school as well. On this day two opposing female gang members attacked each other in full view of the line of waiting voters. One can only imagine how appalled and frightened the voters waiting in line were. Should they interfere, call someone or flee to safety? And where WAS safety?

The school police made the determination that these girls might be candidates for the Longmont Restorative Justice Program, specifically, a special type of conference called a Peacemaking Circle. In this type of circle both girls were treated as offenders and held equally accountable. The girls attended with their parents. The school participated as the victim, voicing its concern about the viability and reputation of the school and the absence of safety within its walls. Also present were the school resource officer, impartial community members familiar with the restorative process and school district personnel, all giving voice to the ripple effects of violence on the school and community as a whole.

It was challenging when one set of parents took a decidedly defensive position while the other set of parents seemed more willing to cooperate in the process. Difficulties were further complicated by the need for Spanish/English translations.

Occasionally tempers flared, but eventually the girls appeared to see the harm in their actions, both to themselves and to the rest of their school.

Much to everyone's surprise the girls agreed, as part of their contracts to repair the harm done, to act as leaders of a second and larger Peacemaking Circle involving both gangs. The focus was finding non-violent solutions to their issues. The school provided authorization and an interventionist was assigned to contact and insure the attendance of approximately 30 members of both gangs.

The first meeting was disastrous. There was a palpable tension as both sides segregated upon entering the room, posturing their animosity with looks and gestures. After introductions the two female leaders shared what they had learned from the Peacemaking Circle, hoping to enlist the participation of the rest of the girls. Because the girls felt they were there only because ordered to do so, they showed no interest and things deteriorated quickly as arguments and accusations between the two gangs created a nasty and threatening atmosphere. One girl exited loudly, the others expressed a desire to leave and the circle was broken.

The following week the school interventionist called saying the gang issue was worse than ever and could something be done – anything, the school was desperate. Once again the girls were convened except this time each gang met separately. The protocol involved listening deeply with no expectations and asking non-gang related questions such as, "What are your dreams?" "What is important to you?" "What kind of life do you want for yourself?" It soon became apparent that meeting separately was key to creating a safe place for the girls' willingness to participate. Progress was slow but the girls attended and participated regularly in their separate groups for the next two years. Yes, once a week for two years!

It was at this time that a young man, highly respected by both gangs, was tragically killed in an accident. Seen as an opening to bring both sides back together, a special Healing Circle was convened with the purpose of honoring and sharing stories of this young man. Soon, the girls were comforting each other, sad memories became humorous, tears became laughter and a miracle happened. Together the girls came to realize the ridiculous and destructive nature of gangs.

At the close of the Healing Circle, the girls wanted to hug each other in one big group hug. They accomplished this by holding hands in a line and spiraling inward until they were compressed into a tight blob of laughing girls. They wanted photos and even decided to meet in the summer for a group picnic. Witnessing this amazing transformation was an indescribably moving experience that would remain in the hearts and memories of all who participated.

Now, years after the close of this powerful Healing Circle, the school has reported an exceptionally high graduation rate among these young women and no revival of gang activity. Some of the girls still check in with their Circle facilitator, sharing special events in their lives.

Sometimes Circles do not turn out as we would like, but sometimes miracles happen!

∞§∞

Relationships – Windows to Wisdom

Restorative justice offers us the tools we need to build solid relationships that are based on mutual respect and then to navigate challenges as they arise. By returning to the traditions of the ancient ones, we can find our way through our relationship challenges. In Tom's story, the young man who slushed the pedestrians with snow, we see his relationship with the Captain, that did not even exist a month before, powerfully transforming this young man's understanding and making him a wiser person. Every relationship is valuable, no matter how insignificant it may first appear, as it is a potential window to wisdom. We just never know where the next relationship may lead us, but it will surely lead us to greater understanding and wisdom, even love, if we respect it and nurture it. When we deeply hold the value and importance in our lives of this first R, Relationship, we have an important key to preventing conflict and to navigating relationship challenges when they inevitably arise.

> **Every relationship is valuable, no matter how insignificant it may first appear, as it is a potential window to wisdom.**

∞§∞

Knowing When to Let Go of Relationships

To this point I have advocated sustaining relationships. However, there are times when it is wise to let go. Domestic violence happens in all economic, social and cultural groups. It happens in the "best of families." It is likely that someone reading this book is experiencing domestic abuse and may not even know it. That may sound outrageous, but I have encountered a number of abused women who had rationalized what was happening to the point they felt what was going on in their home was "normal." It does not serve us to maintain abusive relationships. It is dangerous to continue relationships that contain domestic violence (DV) or dating violence, as they tend to become increasingly violent over time and may be ultimately lethal. Early departure from an abusive relationship increases the likelihood of being able to be free of it. Domestic violence is defined as violence involving intimate partners. It occurs in all social strata, among straight and gay couples, and either the female or the male partner may be the abused one, though the rates of female victims are much higher. Some say that domestic violence toward males is one of the most under-reported crimes due to the embarrassment associated with it.

It is important to understand the warning signs of abuse, so you can determine which relationships are worth doing the work to sustain, strengthen and learn from and which ones we may want to let go. The typical behaviors associated with domestic abuse are physical, sexual and social threats or actions aimed at hurting and demeaning the partner and isolating her or him from friends and family, so she or he may be dominated for the purpose of serving the abuser. These relationships are not built on a foundation of mutual respect and, therefore, have no basis for long-term satisfaction for both parties.

I recently attended a talk given by Don Miguel Ruiz, author of *The Four Agreements*[7]. He said that real love does not restrict your freedom. That may be a good measure of whether or not the relationship is healthy. It is not uncommon for people who are in abusive relationships to fail to recognize the abusive pattern until it is blatantly violent. Everyone should know some basics about relationship violence, and there are numerous websites, like www.helpguide.org, where you may obtain good information. Knowing the warning signs and patterns could save yourself, your friends, acquaintances, or adult children from heartache and injury. There are also many organizations in our communities dedicated to assisting individuals who are in abusive relationships, like women's shelters, which should also be equipped to advise males who are being abused. DV is a complex, highly charged problem that is difficult, if not impossible, to navigate alone; if you know or suspect you are in an abusive relationship, it is important to seek help from one of these nonprofit organizations that specifically work with domestic violence issues for counseling, awareness of legal issues and general support. There is great wisdom in learning to distinguish the relationships that support our growth and should be maintained from the ones that diminish us and need to be relinquished.

∞§∞

TIPS: The Language of Relationship

You have reached the last section of the chapter on the First R, Relationship. Each R chapter ends with TIPS, a section written directly to you, the reader. These sections contain tips for extracting the essential elements of language specific to that R. In each tip the concept is given in bold and discussed. The italicized lines that follow are intended as examples that demonstrate the concepts. In this case, we are looking at Relationship, and we want to explore how to prepare ourselves, and what it sounds like when we talk about a relationship issue in a restorative way. Each of the restorative R's can be used to enhance our joy in life, and this language section is intended to give tips on how to accomplish that. Remember, like any practice, we just keep getting better the more we use it.

- **Do an internal check.** Calm yourself in whatever way works best for you and check in with the emotions you are experiencing. Approaching conflict when you are angry may work, *if* you can express your anger as your own without blaming someone else. Anger often frightens others and makes them more likely to retreat either physically or emotionally. It usually works better if you can approach the matter when you are calm and in charge of your behavior. Here is an example of anger expressed in a way that takes responsibility rather than blaming another:

I am so angry; I should have known better than to behave like that. Now Angela is mad at me, and Greg is in hot water at home, and it's all because of my careless mouth.

- **Ask yourself: what is the value of this relationship?** This refers to your internal dialogue. Before approaching another, remember to check in and get clear about what value this relationship holds in your life. The greater the value, the greater the need to muster the courage needed to work it out. Do not forget that *every* relationship has value, so dig as deep as needed to uncover the levels of value in the relationship that is challenging you.

Greg has been one of my very best friends for thirty years. If I can't find a way to apologize to his wife and still hold my integrity, I will likely lose his friendship or diminish my self-respect, or both. He is someone I have always counted on to be there for me when life got tough. His friendship is of enormous value to me, and I do like her, too, though she probably doesn't believe it.

- **Focus on the person's assets.** Approaching someone when there is conflict can be difficult. It can help if you begin by talking about what you value in the other person and why the relationship matters to you. The assessment of the other's assets must be sincere; false praise or flattery is pretty easy to detect and is likely to do further harm to the relationship. Everybody has good qualities; if you cannot articulate the other's strengths, you aren't ready to approach the problem with her yet. It's really hard not to like someone who appreciates you and recognizes your gifts.

Angela, I see that you are a loyal and committed wife to Greg, and I respect you for that. You are creative and artistic and you've made your home beautiful. I'm glad Greg has found someone who makes him happy, and I see that he truly loves you. I am sorry that my words last week were disrespectful. . . (We'll delve deeper into the fine art of apology in the Repair chapter.)

- **The value of the relationship is the gold standard for measuring your commitment to do the work needed to go beyond the challenges.** Any time the dialogue gets too tough and you or the other party appear ready to give up, revisit the value of the relationship.

Having a good relationship with you matters a lot to me, and not just because of Greg, but also because you're smart and I enjoy talking with you and hearing your opinions. And you've got a great sense of humor, too. What I did was wrong, but I am trying hard to work through this, because your friendship really matters to me. It's too important to just walk away without getting to the bottom of this and making it right.

Chapter 4
A Ripple in the Pond

If we do not have peace in the world, it is because we have forgotten that we belong to each other.

— Mother Teresa

Imagine a large boulder being dropped in a pond; see the immediate splash, and then the ripples flowing out in concentric circles, becoming less intense as they move outward from the point of impact. In restorative justice, we think of crime in much this way. The most direct victim of the crime experiences that immediate splash, and as the ripples move outward, communities, from the local to the global, may experience some level of impact.

The multicultural teaching tale, *Not Our Problem,* helps us appreciate the impact on many others of a single decision by one person.

∞§∞

Not Our Problem: A Tale from Thailand
Retold by Lana Leonard

The King sat with his advisor eating rice cakes with honey. As they ate, they leaned from the open palace window and watched the street below. They talked about this and that. The King, not paying attention to what he was doing, let a drop of honey fall onto the

55

windowsill. "Oh sire, let me wipe that up," offered the advisor. "Never mind," said the King, "It is not our problem, the servants will clean it up later."

As the two continued their conversation, dining on honey and rice, the drop of honey slowly began to drip down the windowsill. Finally, it fell with a plop on the street below. Soon a fly landed on the drop of honey and began his own meal. Immediately a gecko sprang from under the palace and with a flip of its long tongue swallowed the fly. But a cat had seen the gecko and pounced. Then a dog sprang forward and attacked the cat!

"Sire, there seems to be a dog and cat fight in the street. Shouldn't we call someone to stop it?"

"Never mind," said the King. "It is not our problem." The two continued to munch on their honey and rice.

Meanwhile, the cat's owner had arrived and was beating the dog. The dog's owner ran up and began to beat the cat. Soon the two were beating each other.

"Sire, there are two people fighting in the street now. Shouldn't we send someone to break this up?"

The King lazily looked from the window. "Never mind," he said. "It's not our problem."

The friends of the cat's owner gathered and began to cheer him on. The friends of the dog's owner began to cheer her on as well. Soon both groups entered the fight and attacked each other.

"Sire, a number of people are fighting in the street now. Perhaps we should call someone to break this up."

The king was too lazy to even look. You can guess what he said. "Never mind. It's not our problem."

Now soldiers were on the scene. At first they tried to break up the fighting. But when they heard the cause of the fight, some sided with the cat's owner and others sided with the dog's owner. Soon the soldiers too had joined the fight.

With the soldiers involved the fight erupted into civil war. Houses were burned down. Many people were harmed. The palace itself was set on fire and burned to the ground.

The King and his advisor stood surveying the ruins. "Perhaps," said the King, "I was wrong. Perhaps the drop of honey WAS our problem."

∞§∞

We Are All Connected – For Better and For Worse

Mystics of all the world's wisdom traditions espouse the belief that we are all connected. This may be true at the deepest level from a spiritual perspective, and it is also true on the material plane. Humans live in communities and carry out many of our societal function in groups, and ones of our species who do not interact well with others not only get low marks in kindergarten, but are seen as aberrant, dysfunctional, even disturbed. There are exceptions in indigenous society, like the Shuar of Ecuador[8] who traditionally live in single family groups deep in the jungle; even they found it

57

necessary to form bonds of *amikri*, sacred alliances, with others for protection.

Despite all our sophisticated technologies, it is in the ancient systems that we find great hope today. Restorative justice processes were devised for the very purpose of establishing and reestablishing right relationships, and applications of these restorative processes are producing remarkable social results in our modern world.

This book comes with a gift in its hands. It offers the indigenous wisdom that has survived for millennia for how to bring people back into right relationship when the relationship has become stressed or broken, as seems inevitable when we live together.

The ancients understood that no one was expendable. As noted in our first story, the well being, perhaps the very survival, of the tribe depended on everyone's contribution, and a fractionated tribe bode danger, a precarious future. In the practice of restorative justice, I have witnessed many times the ripples of pain and distress being transformed by the process into positive connections that also spread outward to enhance individuals and communities.

∞§∞

Conflict Done Well Builds Stronger Relationships

By learning to manage conflict and address wrongdoing in a restorative way, we can strengthen our world. Our leaders make war across the globe, but individually most of us shrink from engaging in conflict. When I give seminars and trainings and ask participants what they think of when they hear the word "conflict," the vast majority of the words offered up are fear-based — fight, hurt, blood, anger, combat. Rarely do I hear the word that I most

By learning to manage conflict and address wrongdoing in a restorative way, we can strengthen our world.

associate with conflict — opportunity. Relationships can grow greatly through conflict if the conflict is managed constructively.

I believe we have such resistance to conflict because of our wounds from experiencing destructive forms of conflict, and we have not learned the skills for constructively managing it. Both our attitudes and our skills in this area need development. The ancients devised restorative justice to solve problems among people when they arose and to keep the members of the tribe in healthy relationship. Much of it was lost to us when rulers saw ways to profit from creating courts and intervening in the personal affairs of the populace.

> **Relationships can grow greatly through conflict if the conflict is managed constructively.**

Today restorative justice is sweeping the world and enjoying a major revival in criminal justice, in schools, in corporations, in churches, in social services. The principles and values of restorative justice are both robust and elegant, and they may be applied in virtually every arena of human endeavor.

Environmental sustainability is a term we hear often as, more and more, we realize the need to live leaner, on every level, if we are to avoid consuming the very planet we depend upon for life. Restorative justice offers us both content and process to promote sustainability on the social level that we surely need to avoid annihilating each other and to be able to work cooperatively to solve global problems. The terms substantive and procedural refer to different aspects of law. The substantive relates to the substance, the rules, the "thou shalts" — what we cannot do, like homicide; it is the general principle that a court applies in its work. The procedural refers to the processes that must be followed in observance of the law, like how the police must read the Miranda Rights to someone being arrested. The Circle process offers the procedural, guidance for how to conduct the discourse among people so that every voice is heard and considered in arriving at consensus. The 5 R's are the substantive of restorative justice; they tell us what we must and must not do. Operating at both of these levels increases the magnitude of the positive ripples.

∞§∞

This Mother Understood

After a Circle, a mother asked if she could call me the next day. Of course she could, though I had no idea what she wanted. When the call came through early the next morning, she asked if I could give her an outline of how I conducted our Circle and a copy of the 5 R's. She wanted to start doing something like this at home with her family. She was so happy to have found a respectful process that recognized the value of her son and still held him accountable for his behavior. I have since wondered about that ripple. I know how hard it is not *to follow your parents' values, styles and procedures when raising children. A smile comes as I consider how far the positive ripples of that one Circle may go. The seeds are planted for future generations of her family to be held accountable for misbehavior within a context of care. I hope the family history will tell of the time that this mother rewrote the family story by removing violence from their discipline process.*

Another mother, Mother Teresa, said, "If we do not have peace in the world, it is because we have forgotten that we belong to each other." Restorative justice provides a clear and simple road map for the journey back to each other, and the guides are the Circle process and the 5 R's.

Chapter 5
Respect — The Second R

He promised, and urged his fellow Elders to promise, to 'think of the value of the life we are dealing with.'

—Rupert Ross, *Dancing with a Ghost.*

I recall the scene as clearly as this morning's breakfast. My mother, in her nightgown and robe, flinging open the back door. "Jack, Beverly, get in this house right now. The whole neighborhood can hear you. Get IN here RIGHT NOW!" She stomped her foot for emphasis. My father and my 16 year-old willful self were arguing loudly (at least I was loud) about respect. I wasn't showing it in the way he thought appropriate to our relationship, and he was just messing in my life again. When my father and I disagreed, it often came back to the issue of respect. To me his definition of respect was "Do what I say," and anything else was considered disrespectful. Perhaps this principle is especially precious to me, because I've struggled so hard to understand it. Finally, I have come to see that I don't have to surrender my power to respect someone else. Respect is not a win-lose proposition. It has taken me many years to comprehend this.

> **Finally, I have come to see that I don't have to surrender my power to respect someone else. Respect is not a win-lose proposition.**

Respect Keeps It Safe

The quote at the beginning of this chapter suggests the lives we deal with, others and our own, hold value of which we should always be mindful. Respect is the foundation for all restorative practices, as it is what keeps the process safe. In fact, it is what keeps all of our relationships safe and allows us to do conflict constructively. Its importance in restorative practices is emphasized by inclusion in the ground rules for the Circle process. It is essential that all persons in a restorative process be treated with respect and that they extend respect to all other participants and themselves. When we respect ourselves, we do not just go along with the crowd; we speak up for what we believe, and we only tell the truth as best we know it. Respect grants others a measure of dignity just because they are people. It recognizes every human being as a sacred spirit with worth and significance. Respect is given not because of anything that person has done or not done, just because he or she is a person. It is not about respecting others' behavior; it is about respecting their humanity.

> **Respect is the foundation for all restorative practices, as it is what keeps the process safe.**

> **It is not about respecting others' behavior; it is about respecting their humanity.**

Respect for others rests in acknowledging their inherent right to their own perspective, even if it differs from ours. Professor Openshaw admonished my graduate school class to view all knowledge as tentative; it is just the best we know at the moment. It occurred to me one day that I could believe something with all my heart and soul, and then later discover I had been utterly mistaken, absolutely wrong. Ever since that window of understanding opened for me, it has been easier for me to respect other people's opinions, even when they are different from mine. When we integrate this one principle of respect into our way of seeing the world, it immediately eliminates much of our conflict. Another who disagrees with my point of view does not have to be wrong; we simply see it differently — at this moment — and I may even discover later, the other person was the one who had it right!

In one of my favorite books on restorative justice, *Dancing with a Ghost,* [9] Rupert Ross, an assistant Crown's attorney, went to the remote communities of Northern Canada to administer the Queen's justice. There he learned from the First Nations People about another way of doing justice, a more respectful way. These humble people did not promote their ways as superior, but merely held that "Kitchi-Manitou has given us a different understanding." That is precisely the kind of respect that disarms hostility and promotes the offering of respect in kind. Have you noticed that when you smile at strangers, they almost always smile back? Many social interactions follow this Principle of Reciprocity; what you give is what you get, and that is one reason that respect is essential and non-negotiable in a restorative process.

∞§∞

Disrespected Police Officers

We were at a facilitator team meeting. Two police officers came to the meeting because they had been displeased by their experience of a Circle. They had encountered a 16 year-old one evening in a park that had been experiencing a lot of vandalism. He was dressed in dark clothing, and the officers suspected he had been breaking light bulbs in the park. When they attempted to question him, he got belligerent and "mouthy," according to the officer. There was a scuffle in the arrest process, and the young man was put on the ground with his face in the dirt. The young man was indignant, and the officer felt very disrespected. Their sergeant had referred the case to restorative justice.

When we debriefed this case with our volunteer facilitator team, the young officer expressed disappointment that the facilitator had treated this teen with a high level of respect in the Circle, and he questioned why everyone in restorative justice is treated with respect. The officer's evidence against the youth was thin, and had he cooperated with the police at the scene, the event would likely have ended there. In the Circle it was never completely clear if he had or had not vandalized, but the Circle shifted focus to the issue of respect. At one point in the debriefing, the officer said to me, "I know that we didn't have a strong case, but in a normal circle, why would you treat him that respectfully when he was such a punk that night? His behavior was what got him in trouble. Why would you respect him after that?"

The answer was simple. "Only treat him with respect if you never want to see him again. The more he feels like a victimized, devalued person, the greater the likelihood he'll want to give that back to others. And the more he feels honored and respected, the more likely he is to respect others and community property."

We didn't reach a fully satisfying ending in this case, though it did come to an Agreement that was successfully completed. Not every case is tidy and has a magical moment with an empathy breakthrough. But I think that discussion of respect held enormous learning that rippled into a greater understanding for us all. And I hope the young man learned it is never a good idea to disrespect anyone, but especially a police officer.

Neutralizing Shame with Respect

I sometimes think of shame as the evil twin of respect. Shaming may be seen as the opposite of respecting. Much has been written in the field of criminal psychology about the leading role of shame in crime and violence. Donald Nathanson in *Shame and Pride: Affect, Sex, and the Birth of the Self,* [10] forwards nine continua of innate affects (emotions) with shame — humiliation being at the extreme end of the negative affects. He suggests that people use illegal drugs in an attempt to "ameliorate intense noxious affect." [11]

> Being treated with respect in a Circle may help to neutralize the ill effects of shame. By experiencing respect, forgiveness, and empathy, offenders find their way back to self-respect.

Being treated with respect in a Circle may help to neutralize the ill effects of shame. By experiencing respect, forgiveness, and empathy, offenders find their way back to self-respect. When we understand the victim/perpetrator cycle, we recognize that offending most often results from having been victimized. While this does not excuse the offense, it does make it more understandable.

Dr. James Gilligan, in *Violence; Reflections of a National Epidemic,* [11] says that violence is done to discharge shame. Offenders act out of a sense of being victims, and punishment does not work, because it reinforces their victim status. The restorative justice approach *requires* that everyone be treated with respect, regardless of

> Offenders act out of a sense of being victims, and punishment does not work, because it reinforces their victim status.

how we perceive their behavior. In fact, it may be that the more offensive the behavior, the greater the need for exhibiting respect for the person, so there can be an opening for redirecting that behavior. Understanding these concepts makes me cringe when I overhear a parent shaming a child for his behavior; with just a little tweak of understanding, the behavior could be redirected and the problem solved instead of the child being shamed and potentially damaged.

∞§∞

Saving Face

Respect is an abstract concept, and yet it is important enough that many a man lost his life in a duel because his honor was disrespected. Such lethal confrontations over honor are not only from the Age of Chivalry; they persist today. The rules may have changed, but the outcome has not shifted much. In gang parlance, one of the absolute challenges that cannot be left unanswered is to "dis" another. A newspaper recounted the story of a young Denver gang banger who had shot and killed another youth. When the police asked him why he did it, he replied, "I had to kill him, he gave me the look." "The look" refers to a non-verbal show of disrespect, sometimes called "mad dogging" or "mugging."

One of the cardinal principles of conflict resolution is that people must have a way to save face. Face saving in conflict is essential; for people to be able to resolve the problem, they need a way to do so with honor. There are strong, longstanding values around challenging a person's honor, or treating them with disrespect; it is a sure way to escalate a conflict, perhaps

If offering respect to another person opens the door to the possibility of a mutually satisfying resolution to a problem, it seems a small gesture with a huge potential for reward.

66

even to a death fight. Indulging in signs of disrespect may feel powerful and justified in the moment but will rarely move toward long term, positive solution, and will more likely lead to an escalation of pain. If offering respect to another person opens the door to the possibility of a mutually satisfying resolution of a problem, it seems a small gesture with a huge potential for reward.

∞§∞

Listening to Understand

An important way to show respect is to fully listen to someone. All too often we listen to others while primarily scanning their content for the focus of our response. We are not so much listening to them as formulating our reply. Restorative processes require deep listening done in a way that does not presume we know what the speaker is going to say, but honoring the importance of the other's point of view. In RJ the focus for listening is to understand other people, to see their point, not to make our own point or even to judge their perspectives — just simply listening to understand them. When we really listen to them, even if we disagree with their thinking, we can be respectful and try hard to comprehend how it appears to them.

Circle talking is designed to support this kind of careful listening. In the Circle, speaking and listening is not a back and forth process like we typically experience in everyday life. Each person has his or her turn to speak without interruption; you do not get to challenge the speaker's thinking or

> **In the Gandhian perspective of conflict, "opponents" are viewed as fellow truth seekers, and the task at hand is to discern a higher truth that allows for both sides' understanding to be honored.**

respond in any way until it is your turn. By then, what is on your mind will have shifted several times, and only the most pertinent points are likely to remain and be spoken. More often than not, when it is their turn to speak, people voice their own perspective rather than responding to others. Back and forth dialogue can quickly degenerate to bickering, but Circle talking more often leads to understanding. Sometimes in Circle, the facilitator may provide an opportunity for questions. The purpose of these questions is to explore, not to cross-examine. We ask questions not to challenge another's belief but to seek to understand it more fully. It serves us well to consider the act of listening as a search for wisdom. In the Gandhian perspective of conflict, "opponents" are viewed as fellow truth seekers, and the task at hand is to discern a higher truth that allows for both sides' understanding to be honored.

Another important lesson about respect came to me from my husband:

A few years after my husband and I were married, we needed to make an important decision. We researched the issues, weighed the pros and cons and sat down to discuss what we should do. After talking through all the points we could think of, he said he needed to call his parents. At the time even the cost of a long distance call was not insignificant to us, and I couldn't imagine what points they could make that we hadn't already considered, but he was insistent. When I pushed him a bit more, he dropped the bomb on me, the "R" word; he insisted it was the respectful thing to do. He called. I was right; they didn't have any new thinking to add, and he was also right. Even if they didn't have anything more to add that time, they might have, and, more importantly, it was the respectful thing to do.

∞§∞

Expressing Anger

Fully listening to another is one of the greatest gestures of respect — trying on what the other says, not listening to defend, to build an argument for your point of view. Listening fully before responding pays the greatest respect to the other person. And when we honor another in that way, it will likely be given back in return. If not, it is fair to ask for it. Sometimes people just have not had enough experience with this kind of respect to reciprocate without prompting.

I am often asked about how it works in Circle when people are angry. It is possible, even healthy, for honest anger to be present, if the anger is expressed in ways that are respectful of all other parties. The facilitator may need to help an angry participant do this well. Appropriate expression of anger needs to be voiced as a first person point of view from the speaker's perspective. It is not okay to point fingers at others, because those accusations can only be based in assumptions that may or may not be accurate. When we speak from our own point of view, we can be sure that our assumptions are true and honest. The "I" statement we learned in basic communications class serves this purpose well.

Formula: I feel/felt _(describe the feeling)_ when _(describe the act or word or event, etc., that induced the feeling)_, because _(describe how you were impacted)_ .

Example: I felt _so angry I wanted to scream_ when _I saw that my car had been keyed_, because _it felt like an attack on me, like someone had scratched big gashes all over my face_.

Note that an "I" statement never contains the word "you." "I got angry when you. . ." is _not_ an "I" statement.

69

This kind of expression of anger can help the Circle to appreciate the harm that has been done, and it can also be empathy enhancing for the offender who is internally recognizing she had a role in causing this pain to another. That is precisely the reason that RJ is not a good process to use with persons who have certain personality disorders and have limited capacity for empathy. Under the right circumstances, persons who bully can benefit from a Circle. I am cautious with using Circles in cases of bullying, because those who bully may actually enjoy causing pain in others, and it would be unethical to have a victim reveal their vulnerabilities to someone who may use that information to cause further injury in the future. This is a good example of the reason preconference assessments are essential to the ethical use of formal restorative practices.

The Circle Is Good at Discerning Truth

Truth is another subject that often comes up around discussions of respect. People find it much easier to give respect when they believe that the other person is telling the truth. Often in RJ, new facilitators put a lot of emphasis on whether or not someone, usually an offender, is being fully honest in the telling of their story. They presume that there is one definitive truth and the whole Circle hinges on that person coming completely clean. While confession is good for the soul, and nothing can bring compassion to a Circle faster than a completely honest and remorseful story, the Circle has sophisticated radar and is capable of discerning honesty.

In *Made for Each Other*[12], Meg Olmert discusses nonverbal communication. She cites psychologist Paul Ekman who spent seven years studying human faces for non-verbal language. "He's proven that all over the world – from Winnipeg to Borneo – people make the same faces and they mean the same thing." At some level, we are all able to discern the meaning and trustworthiness of the storyteller in a Circle, regardless of language and cultural differences. When I'm facilitating, I do not fret too much over how much truth is Truth; I trust that to the wisdom of the Circle. Remember, the facilitator's job is to conduct the process and maintain a safe container; the participants' job is to wrestle the tough issues and provide the content for the Circle. After all, Truth has many faces.

There is no better illustration of the many faces of Truth than this story that comes to us from Rumi, the great 13th century mystic of Balkah, now Afghanistan.

The Blind Ones and the Elephant
As Retold by Lana S. Leonard

Beyond Ghor there was a city. All its inhabitants were blind. A king with his entourage arrived near by; he brought his army and camped in the desert. He had a mighty elephant that he used in attacks to increase the people's awe.

The people became anxious to see the elephant and some sightless ones from among this blind community ran like fools to find it. As they did not know either the form or shape of an elephant, they groped sightlessly, gathering information by touching some part of it. Each thought that he knew something, because he could feel a part of the huge beast.

When they returned to their fellow citizens, eager groups clustered around them, each of these was anxious, misguidedly, to learn the truth from those who themselves did not know the whole truth. They asked about the form, the shape of the elephant, and they listened to everything that was said. The man whose hand had reached an ear was asked about the elephant's nature. He said, "It is a large, rough thing, wide and broad like a rug."

And the one who had felt the trunk said, "I have the real facts about it. It is like a straight and hollow pipe, full of power and destructive."

The one who had felt its feet and legs said, "It is tall, mighty and firm like a pillar."

Each had felt only one part out of many. Each had perceived it wrongly. No one knew all. All imagined something, something incorrect.

When all voices of the Circle join together in sharing their perspectives and deeply listening to each other, it is possible to find the important truth.

∞§∞

Wounding Begets Wounding: The Victim-Perpetrator Cycle

It is easy to hear a story and decide just what someone *should* have done. It may also be arrogant to believe that we know what is best for someone else, as we all have to learn our lessons in our own way. People are who they need to be to attract the lessons this life has for them. We can only advance and grow when our experience is sufficient to support that next step. Those choices must be made only for ourselves. At 16 years of age, I could not hear my father's wisdom that now seems so clear to me. However, we should not do nothing, just sit back and offer no assistance to someone who is struggling and making choices that hurt himself and others.

72

It helps to understand the victim-perpetrator cycle. When someone has been victimized, he is prone to do that kind of thing to another person. It is that Reciprocity Principle again. When we encounter others who cause pain, if they feel safe enough to tell us their stories, and if we listen deeply, we will find the pain that was previously done to them. Sometimes people cause harm out of negligence or recklessness, but it usually comes as a response to their own pain. Henry Wadsworth Longfellow wrote, "If we could read the secret history of our 'enemies', we should find in each one's life sorrow and suffering enough to disarm all hostility."

> **Sometimes people cause harm out of negligence or recklessness, but it usually comes as a response to their own pain.**

The simple act of deep listening and of expressing empathy to others, as described by Marshall Rosenberg in his system of Non-violent Communication, can be a balm for our soul's wounds. In his book *Nonviolent Communication: a language of life* [13], he devotes a chapter to the power of empathy, discussing its capacity to heal. He further recognizes the need for us to connect compassionately with ourselves and gives lessons on how to forgive ourselves.

A great beauty of restorative justice is that by listening to others' stories in the safety of the Circle, our compassionate hearts are opened. A compassionate heart provides the perfect setting for respecting the person while expecting accountability for harm caused to self and others. It is this very combination that accounts for RJ's success – firm accountability within a

> **It is this very combination that accounts for RJ's success – firm accountability within a context of care, not just a gratuitous, do-gooder kind of care, but a sincere regard grounded in the understanding of the offender's woundedness.**

context of care, not just a gratuitous, do-gooder kind of care, but a sincere regard grounded in the understanding of the offender's woundedness. I have left this kind of Circle many times feeling like a better human being, that my higher human emotions have gotten good exercise and are stronger for it.

$$\infty\S\infty$$

A Father's Compassionate Heart

I was facilitating a Circle for a very young boy, Sam, who had seriously injured a smaller boy, Matt, on the playground at an elementary school. Sam was new to the school and was not being well accepted by the other boys. Sam was large for his age and very physical. His single mother was working long, hard hours to provide for her children who were home alone a lot. Sam had been surrounded on the playground that day by a group of taunting boys. Even though he was much larger than any one of them, he was frightened by the group, so he picked up the smallest boy, Matt, and executed a pile driver move he had seen on a wrestling show on television. Matt's neck was broken, but because he was young, he was not permanently disabled. However, his injuries were quite serious, and he had severe headaches and had to wear a halo brace for months. Matt's parents came to the Circle very angry.

After many tears and anguish in the story telling, it was time to start the Agreement phase. Sam's assets review revealed that he wanted to play sports, especially football, and the Circle recognized that this boy desperately needed a physical outlet for his strength and a positive way to connect with the other boys. His mom said that she couldn't afford the fees, let alone the uniform and equipment needed. Everyone in the

Circle understood that this mother and her son were struggling on many levels, and without help, their prospects were dim. Their lack of resources seemed to prohibit the very thing that was needed.

As I sat with silence in the Circle wondering where to go next, Matt's father spoke up. "I coach a city league football team for Sam's age group. You bring him down to Watts Park next Saturday morning, and I'll suit him up." I could hardly believe my ears as I witnessed this man who had, a short time earlier, been ready to throttle this very boy he was now throwing a lifeline. This may have been the first time, but not the last, that I've had tears rolling down my face as I continued to do my facilitator's job. There have been many, many times since when I have thought of that time and how proud I felt to witness this profound moment and this valiant man who had a heart large enough to care for his own son and still find room to help another suffering boy with no father.

∞§∞

Everyone Has to Make Their Choices

So, if it is arrogant to think we know what another should do, can we offer advice that is respectful? As we saw in the previous story, there are certainly respectful ways we can reach out and help. We can also help by bearing witness to another's life and reflecting on what we have learned from our experience. Not telling them what they should do, but by sharing what we have learned from related or similar life experiences and the choices, both good and bad, that we made. If we do this with deep appreciation for who they are and their right to choose for their own life, they are left to "try on" what has been shared to see if it might make sense for

75

them. They need to feel free to choose without judgment of their choices, not obliged to comply with our point of view.

I encountered three generations of a family whose belief system was causing many problems in their lives. After listening to story after story of their difficulties with others and "the system," I became concerned that a single, long-held family belief was repeatedly at the source of their problem. Their family belief held that "Men have to settle their problems like men, the old fashioned way." When I asked what that meant exactly, I got euphemisms, like "take it outside" or "settle it behind the barn" instead of straight answers. After much listening and careful consideration of their perspective, I asked the grandfather how that belief is serving his family now and how might it serve their future generations. Assuming the grandfather only wants to pass along wisdom that will strengthen his family, it seemed a fair question to ask him to consider how it is serving his family today, as his grandson was about to be expelled from school for fighting. I do not know if my questions changed anything for him or not, but at least he had the opportunity to consider another perspective. He gets to choose. I felt that was the most respectful thing I could do for this family.

From restorative justice guidance and a little help from my friends, this is what I have come to understand about the meaning of respect. I show respect for myself by speaking my truth gently and from my own point of view, while understanding that truth is rarely absolute. Truth is perceived through our individual lenses of culture and life experience. Respect for others involves honoring their humanity and listening to them with an open mind and an open heart. Respect means carefully considering the other's point of view, and all the while treating it as a search for wisdom. Respect is best given to yourself and others in a gentle way — not with a loud voice. Finally, Papa Jack, my dear father, I get it!

TIPS: The Language of Respect

- **Show non-verbal signs of respectful listening**. Leaning toward a person, making soft eye contact, nodding are ways to show you are considering another's point of view. Check yourself that you are not eye rolling, sitting with arms tightly folded over the chest in a closed position, fidgeting or giving other nonverbal signals of impatience or dissent.

- **Use the Principle of Reciprocity.** Think about what you want, and then offer it to the other person first; it's like the Golden Rule. "Do unto others as you would have them do unto you," with one concept added. If you do it to them first, they will more likely do it back to you.

- **Demonstrate respect to children**. When a child is trying to tell you something, the most respectful thing an adult can to is to stop what he/she is doing, get on the child's level, make eye contact and say, "What you have to say is important to me. I am listening." This is not always possible, but it should not be an uncommon experience for a child.

- **Use respectful questions.** "Can you help me understand?" This is one of my favorite questions for teens, and it works with any age group. It implies that they are understandable and that you care to take the time to understand them. Another favorite is, "Why am I having so much trouble believing this?" A common response is to tell me what they had left out that makes the story hang together. Notice the phrasing; it does not say they are doing anything wrong or deceitful, but suggests that the trouble is with me.

77

- **Honor his responsibility for his life**. I do not know what is right for you to do; you are the one who can best decide that. What are your choices? If you did this one what do you think would happen? What about that one? What seems to be the option that is most likely to get you where you want to go?

- **Show you value her life**. "I'd like to get to know you" may be the highest compliment we can pay another. As we express positive regard for her, we show that we respect and value her life.

$\infty\S\infty$

Chapter 6
The Restorative Way

There is no way to peace. Peace is the way.

—A.J. Muste

In his groundbreaking book, *Changing Lenses*, [14] Howard Zehr defines restorative justice by saying, "Crime is a violation of people and relationships. It creates obligations to make things right. Justice involves the victim, the offender, and the community in a search for solutions which promote repair, reconciliation, and reassurance."

He contrasts this to retributive justice where, "Crime is a violation of the state, defined by lawbreaking and guilt. Justice determines blame and administers pain in a contest between the offender and the state directed by systematic rules." Zehr devised three questions that effectively

> **By contrast restorative justice asks three very different questions: What harm was done; what needs to be done to repair the harm; and who is responsible for the repair?**

and succinctly distinguish retributive and restorative justice. When a crime has been committed, retributive justice asks these questions: What law was broken; who broke the law; and how shall we punish the offender? By contrast restorative justice asks three very

79

different questions: What harm was done; what needs to be done to repair the harm; and who is responsible for the repair?

Imagine that you, or your best friend, committed a crime. Which form of justice would you hope to have applied to the case? Many people equate the term justice to being tough on crime, and they want harsh punishments, until they find themselves facing that system. We have experienced many crime victims who say the most important thing to them is to be able to face their perpetrator and tell them how their lives were affected by what that person did. I recall being at a RJ conference in Vancouver, BC, with a man from Fresno State University who used the slogan, "Restorative justice is what the people want." It seems so true as evidenced by the satisfaction ratings from our Circles being 95% or higher for all participant groups: victims, offenders, parents, supporters, police, other professionals, community members.

∞§∞

A New Way of Thinking About Punishment

The restorative way requires a paradigm shift in the way we think about punishment. Restorative justice relies on individuals to accept personal responsibility for the effects of their behavior and the needed repair rather than using externally applied punishment for the wrongdoing. When we punish, the ideal is to administer an amount of pain that is equal to the amount of damage done, as if two wrongs could make a right. The concept of an eye for an eye was actually forwarded to address the need for "just" punishment that is not overly harsh. However, Gandhi pointed out, "An eye for an eye and the whole world is blind."

The adage "Spare the rod and spoil the child" even *sounds* mean-spirited. Many people cling to the belief that wrongdoing should be punished, and they reject the restorative way and believe anything that is not punitive is soft. Punishment has been the subject of much research and a lot has been written about it that may be explored in other sources. The aspect that appears to me most relevant to our discussion lies in the external vs. internal locus of control.

An emotionally healthy individual does not want to be in charge of others' lives. She recognizes that being in charge of her own life and doing that well is difficult enough, yet we cannot administer punishment without taking charge of another's life. Everything operates more smoothly when individuals are expected to be responsible for themselves. One of the most common laments among school teachers is often spoken in a frustrated tone. "These kids just don't take responsibility for their own behavior!" And it is really not that much different with adults, I find. Think what a lovely world it might be if *everyone* did that one thing!

This ideal might not be achievable, because we may always need protection from the low empathy folks who find satisfaction in hurting others. We may always need prison guards and others to manage our safety. However, we could greatly increase the numbers of self-responsible adults if

> **We need to teach children what accountability involves, expect it of them and reward them when they demonstrate it.**

we would exchange punishment for accountability. We need to teach children what accountability involves, expect it of them and reward them when they demonstrate it. And this practice applies just as well as an internal process as an external one. We punish and denigrate ourselves when we would be better served by examining the harm that resulted from our behavior and repairing it. We need to treat our mistakes as lessons to learn from rather than as fodder for negative self-talk.

One way to encourage self-responsibility is to expect it. A vast body of education research shows that students tend to meet the expectation their teachers hold for them, referred to as the

Pygmalion Effect. When kids have broken a rule or are in conflict or crisis, adults are quick to jump in and dictate a punishment or solution, and, unwittingly, give kids the message that they do not have to be responsible for themselves. Think how much better it would be if those same adults took charge by separating the kids, if needed, for safety or cooling down, and then telling them that they have to figure out how their behavior has hurt each other and then fix it. They could come out of "time out," for example, when they had figured that out. Telling others what they should do is rarely well received, especially by teens.

When I was teaching alternative school teens, their parents would ask me why their children would listen to me and not to them. Besides not being their parent, I do believe the main reason was I did not try to tell them what they should do. Instead, I would engage them in the process of exploring their options and considering the most likely outcomes of the various choices. I would tell them that this is what's involved in creating your own life story; as you make the choices, it may not be so much about what's right and wrong, though it sometimes is, but more often it is just a matter of some doors closing and others opening. And the path leads from one set of choices to the next, all the while creating your life story. You can be the hero of your own

> **You can be the hero of your own story or the victim of someone else's. When we do the inner work to evaluate and make conscious choices, we are acting as the hero, the author of our life story; when we do not, we are primed to be unconscious victims in someone else's story.**

story or the victim of someone else's. When we do the inner work to evaluate and make conscious choices, we are acting as the hero, the author of our life story; when we do not, we are primed to be unconscious victims in someone else's story. (*Victim or Hero, writing your own life story* by Lana Leonard and Beverly Title. This is a sentence completion and personal story writing workbook available at www.lcjp.org)

More and more schools in the United States and elsewhere are shifting away from the top down authority, punishment-oriented discipline system, and they are getting impressive results. The International Institute of Restorative Practices website (www.iirp.org) has a library containing numerous articles about schools that are adopting restorative practices. A chart in the Appendices of this book compares the punitive and restorative approaches to school discipline. The "sex, love and rock and roll" generation of the 60's broke the power of top down authority when they "dropped out," thereby discounting the value of the reward for compliance. Ensuing generations and their parents, and their teachers, have been less willing to accept authority without question, and they have been more responsive to educational models that emphasize student engagement, whether in academic instruction or in school discipline. Though this shift has created some painful ripples, it may be seen as an essential step on our evolutionary journey and has the positive effect of shifting the discipline paradigm away from externally imposed punishment and toward restorative discipline and other models based in self-responsibility.

We do not have to look too deep before we see how broadly the principle of self-responsibility applies, not only to our criminal justice system, but also to the ways in which we administer discipline at home and in schools. Retributive justice was the construct that ruled with my parents who were loving people trying their best to be good parents, to do their duty no matter how much it hurt them — or me. But it did not put me in charge of my own life and teach me how to navigate that responsibility. What it did teach me was that as long as I was clever and deceitful enough, I could do anything I wanted and avoid punishment. This is not a good lesson, especially for a smart kid.

I was in my mid-20's before it occurred to me that I no longer had to lie to anyone about anything. I was an adult now, in charge of my own life. Others could approve or disapprove of my choices, but they were mine to make. The only person whose approval was absolutely non-negotiable was me, and I no longer wanted to speak anything but the truth as I understood it. My parents and my schoolteachers would have had much easier jobs had they taught me the 5 R's and to be accountable for my behavior instead of trying to force me to conform and punish me into compliance.

∞§∞

Teaching Self Responsibility to Children

There are some important keys to teaching accountability. First, there needs to be an atmosphere of respect so that the child does not feel she is risking loss of parental affection by admitting responsibility. It needs to be posed to the child as "an honorable thing to do," that might sound like this, "*A really mature, cool kid knows she is better off to admit her mistakes and then clean up any mess that she caused. I really respect and admire people who are smart enough to do that no matter what age they are.*" It is great to take advantage of opportunities to say things like this when stories appear in real life, not when the child is "in trouble." If you look for such occurrences, they are there. Then, when the child does something that causes harm, you can remind her of how cool that person was in handling the same kind of situation.

> **In our restorative justice practice, there is a carrot (the wrongdoer gets a voice in the repair agreement) and a stick (the case can go back to the police.)**

The next step is very important; ask the child what she might be able to do to make things right. If necessary, brainstorm possibilities with her, but be sure that she is the one to finally decide. Personal choice is one of the most empowering strategies in existence.

In our restorative justice practice, there is a carrot (the wrongdoer gets a voice in the repair agreement) and a stick (the case can go back to the police.) Especially when this is a new process, some children will need the stick to encourage them toward self-responsibility. In such cases, the parent may need to suggest an unsavory consequence (no television, no hockey, etc.) as an alternative to being accountable and repairing harm, until this new way becomes the norm. *If you're not old enough yet to figure out what you need to do, then I'll just have to take over and impose a consequence.* Most children catch on pretty quickly. The parent may need to assist with determining the fairness to all parties of the repair items and then monitoring to see that all agreements are completed. It can be helpful to put agreement items in writing for the child and you to sign. Memory can be such a tricky thing. When agreements are completed, do not forget to celebrate the child's success at being good to her word. Sometimes the most important recognition is a smile and "I'm so proud of you!"

Restorative Justice is Voluntary

Another principle of the restorative way is that participation should be voluntary. The Circle has no evidentiary process and does not determine guilt or innocence. It is only appropriate for those who are able to accept some level of responsibility for their crime and are willing to take direct action to repair the harm. For the criminal offenders I have worked with, participating in restorative justice was a choice, though generally a lesser of evils choice. Some people have questioned the value of participation that is less than whole hearted, but many times Circles begin with the offenders' understanding of the impact of their behavior and their empathy for the victim at a very low level, and then grow to profound levels by the end. When people with capacity for relationship with others witness another's pain, especially if they had a hand in causing it, they experience feelings of empathy as a side effect of the restorative process.

The restorative way should be voluntary for victims also. Our police officers commonly consult victims before making a referral to restorative justice; however, not all victims choose to participate when we contact them. Some say they have moved on and do not want to dredge it up again, or they may be too embarrassed to participate. In those cases we may ask if they would agree to the Circle being held using a surrogate to tell their story. Some practitioners do not support the use of surrogate victims, but I have seen cases where a surrogate was much better able to represent the victim's story than the actual victim could have, as in the case of the young girl told in Chapter Two who was being sexually harassed by the teenage boys at school. We seriously wanted to hold this circle because the life consequences of being labeled a sex offender in "the system" are egregious, yet these teens needed to get a strong message that their behavior had crossed a line. The topic was too mortifying for the young victim who refused to attend, but her mother was brilliant in the Circle, and the outcome was what we had hoped for.

Accountability at the Lowest Level

Some offenders have already understood their harmful behavior before they ever got to the Circle and have decided to make different future choices. Others get it when they hear victims' stories of how their lives have been painfully impacted. Some come to understand through a service "opportunity" they perform as a part of their Circle agreement, like the young man who slushed the pedestrians with snow, and still others' hearts are not opened by the experience at all. When police officers express concerns about "those" kids coming to restorative justice, I tell them, "Don't worry. If it doesn't have the desired impact, you'll get another chance to send her to the system, and it probably won't take very long."

Holding offenders accountable at the lowest level is the most important thing we can do to help them make better future choices. There is significant research to support this statement, but a delinquent teen taught it to me.

> *"Teach, it's like this. When you do risky stuff, especially if it's bad, it's a big rush. And when you get away with it, you just want to do bigger and badder stuff – for the adrenaline and to see what you can get away with. The more you get away with, the more you want to do."*

It was a statement of his raw truth, and, at that moment, I had a profound paradigm shift. I realized that my tender heart that wanted to protect these kids was absolutely doing them harm. The highest, most loving thing I could do for them was to hold them accountable THE FIRST TIME for their behavior, not to let bad behavior go unnoticed. It forever changed how I work with students.

∞§∞

Restorative Justice Strengthens Empathy

As I mentioned earlier, RJ enhances empathy. In a television show about the making of the movie *Munich,* Stephen Spielberg

Empathy differs from sympathy in that it does not require that we feel bad or sad for others, but simply that we have a sense of understanding what it feels like to be them in that moment.

said, "You cannot understand the human motivation without empathy." Empathy differs from sympathy in that it does not require that we feel bad or sad for others, but simply that we have a sense of understanding what it feels like to be them in that moment. Native Americans express it as knowing the feel of another's moccasins. This is the essential quality that allows us to form those all-important bonds of relationship with others. When the other is someone of a similar culture and background it is a simpler process.

I learned a valuable lesson from my sister–in–law one day. Her husband was talking about someone who was coming to their home to work on a project with him. She asked him if the woman was Jewish. Not being Jewish, and being a sometimes-outsider-feeling-person in the rear of the car, I snapped back with, "And what difference does that make" to which she wisely replied, "Well, it will take me longer to get to know her if she's not." I was humbled by her response and, later, appreciative of the lesson.

Restorative justice rests on having some capacity for "feeling another's feelings," and it is not well suited for use with unattached kids. Ken Magid and Carole McKelvey, in their book, *High Risk: Children Without a Conscience*,[15] pointed out that empathy is not a yes or no question, but a continuum. They suggest that you imagine an empathy scale as a line with Mother Theresa and Albert Schweitzer on one end and Adolph Hitler and Charles Manson on the other, and consider that all of us fall somewhere in between. Educators, counselors and nurses, among others, naturally tend toward the higher end of the empathy scale, and they make good community members in a Circle if they also understand the need for firm accountability. Letting someone off easy because you are empathetic does not serve them well, or your community.

I recall reading a newspaper account about a teenage girl who had stolen a car and hit and killed a man who was riding a bicycle. When handing down her sentence, the judge said that his sentence may appear harsh, but it was important that she have a serious enough consequence for this act, so she could put this event behind her when she completed it. Had she felt she got off easy, it would likely have haunted her for the rest of her life. In restorative justice one of the most serious jobs of the Circle is to decide how much is enough and how much is too much. The more neutral community members have great value in that role, especially youth community members.

RJ is not therapy, though the process may be therapeutic for everyone in the Circle. The Circle does not dig for motives; rather it seeks to understand from another's point of view, to stand in his moccasins, and in putting yourself in that place, you exercise your higher emotions like empathy and compassion. Regularly when I am in Circle, I realize that tonight I am the facilitator, but I am no different from anyone else here; on another night, I could have any other role. The Circle connects us to each other; its shape defies hierarchy and suggests infinity. On every plane, we are all connected, and it is a great privilege to regularly be in Circle and be reminded of my humanity and the common bond that joins us to one another.

> **The Circle connects us to each other; its shape defies hierarchy and suggests infinity.**

Restorative Justice Is Not Just for Juvenile, First-Time Offenders

Most restorative justice programs in the United States are for juveniles and are often limited to first offenders. Originally LCJP only took juvenile referrals, but success rates were strong and it was not long before we were asked to take cases with adult offenders as well. LCJP now takes any offenders who accept responsibility for their crimes and agree to repair harm, regardless of their age or crime, but our referral rates for juveniles consistently remain much higher than referral rates for adults. There are, however, some crimes that do not get referred to LCJP, most notably domestic violence and sexual assault.

We have found RJ to be equally effective in addressing felony cases as it is with misdemeanors. Whether or not RJ "works" has little to do with the type of crime or the ages of the persons; what it really has to do with is the parties' capacity for empathy. Recent research suggests that RJ may be even more effective with more serious crimes. Tom Quinn, Director of Probation Services, Colorado Judicial Branch, and an original member of Colorado Restorative Justice Council shared this observation with me. "I can tell you that it is my experience sitting on panels with victims of more serious crimes, even surviving relatives of homicide victims, that they have a lot of "why" questions, and other important questions that are not answered in the adversarial system, but can be more fully put to rest with restorative justice." Once again, we see why it makes sense to be more than offender-focused in our quest for justice. Victims and community members also deserve to have their needs met so they may heal and move on with their lives.

Mark Umbreit of the University of Minnesota is a leader in the United States in using a restorative process to address very serious crimes. He comes from a social work background and has a profound interest in the opportunity that restorative justice brings for healing the crime victims as well as their offenders. Canadian David L. Gustafson also specializes in high-risk dialog, as it is called when there is serious injury or death associated with the case. He bravely facilitates Circles that address sexual abuse and domestic violence. These men are courageous and their work is truly magnificent in the kind of healing outcomes that grow from their work.

∞§∞

The Community Member Role in the Circle

When our original team of eight was first trained to facilitate restorative justice, community members acted as facilitators, and we did not have another role for community in the Circle. We knew that community participation was a restorative value, but we were not sure how to integrate that. It had not been a part of our initial training to conduct Family Group Conferences, a restorative model that brings the victim group and the offender group together with a facilitator, often a police officer.

In indigenous communities, everyone was a community member, but we were bringing people together who had never even met before the Circle. With the help of the Balanced and Restorative Justice (BARJ) Project and discussions with Dennis Maloney of Bend, Oregon, Gordon Bazemore and Mara Schiff of Florida Atlantic University and Mike Dooley of the Department of Corrections Training Center, we increased our understanding of the need to have a balance of all three voices — Victim, Offender, and Community — in our Circles.

We decided to seat Community as an entity in the Circle with individuals representing the impact of a crime on the community and focusing on what needed to be in the Agreement to repair community harm. In the early days we called these folks "Affected Community," and we sought out persons who were perhaps in the first wave of the ripple effect of the crime, like the neighbor of a park that had been vandalized. There was benefit from this voice in the Circle, but these voices were more closely aligned with the victim voice which could tip the Circle out of balance. We had learned from the BARJ project of the need for balance among voices

Community members can function as a neutral third party to the conflict.

of Victim, Community and Offender for the restorative process to do its work well. As we did many such Circles, our concept matured about how the community could best be represented.

Eventually, we dropped the word "Affected," and we now seek people who are community-oriented, but have no inherent affiliation with either the victim or the offender in the Circle. Community members can function as a neutral third party to the conflict. We train them to build a bridge of relationship to the offender, and let him know the community values his life and his community wants him. After that has been communicated, it is time to balance the message so that the expectation of accountability is clear and the need to make repair is taken seriously.

Olmert, in *Made for Each Other,*[16] tells the story of Hans, a clever German horse, whose owner thought he had taught his horse language, music and numbers which Hans demonstrated most convincingly by "answering" questions. However, when researchers probed deeply enough, they found that Hans was providing answers based on non-verbal cues he picked up from observing the human questioners rather than from his own understanding of the questions. And most importantly, "Hans performed best with those humans who had a sincere interest in his success." I doubt that humans are much different in that regard. Many times I've experienced a similar phenomenon in children who only perform well in school if they *believe* the teacher likes them.

> *I recall the Circle for a young boy who was stealing from classmates in his elementary school. From the time they entered the room, his mother was stern and demanding. Sit up straight; take your coat off; stop fidgeting! The boy slumped into his chair, pulled his hood over his face and despite his mother's best efforts to "jerk him up" he wouldn't emerge. As the facilitator of the Circle, I knew I needed to act. This Circle had a preponderance of elementary educators, folks who tend to range toward the high end of the empathy scale, so I felt safe to*

engage their help. I asked that we begin by focusing on what we appreciated about "Johnny." I intentionally started with the school counselor, a kind-hearted woman I was sure would model this appreciative approach well. And she did. As we proceeded around the Circle, even the mother softened and contributed positives about her son. About the time we reached the semicircle point, Johnny emerged from his hood, sat up in his chair, and began to make eye contact with those who were seeing him.

In the introduction to *To Know As We Are Known: Education as a Spiritual Journey,*[17] Parker Palmer writes,

"Many of us live one-eyed lives. We rely largely on the eye of the mind to form our image of reality. But today more and more of us are opening the other eye, the eye of the heart, looking for realities to which the mind's eye is blind. Either eye alone is not enough. We need 'wholesight,' a vision of the world in which mind and heart unite 'as my two eyes make one in sight.' Our seeing shapes our being. Only as we see whole can we and our world be whole."

Everyone needs others to see their gifts and recognize their significance, and community members serve that role in the Circle. The ideal community member brings "wholesightedness" to the Circle.

We Need Both Restorative Justice and Criminal Justice

In my enthusiasm for restorative justice, I sometimes unintentionally give an impression of disrespect for the criminal justice system. I want to be clear that I do not advocate replacing our current justice system with a restorative one, except maybe at the municipal level. To embrace RJ does not exclude the value of our current system. The courts have played a critical role, for example, in the accomplishments of the civil rights movement and in protecting victims of domestic abuse. Those who are falsely accused must have a place where they can prove their innocence. Unfortunately, there are those in our society who refuse to live by the social compact, and our communities must be protected from them. Justice is better served when both systems work together cooperatively and respectfully, honoring the benefits that both can bring.

Chapter 7
Responsibility - The Third R

When you plant lettuce, if it does not grow well, you don't blame the lettuce. You look into the reasons it is not doing well. It may need fertilizer, or more water, or less sun. You never blame the lettuce.

—Thich Nhat Hanh

Too often in our society, we hear people blaming others for what's going wrong. For restorative practices to be effective, persons need to take responsibility for the behavior that caused harm. RJ rests on the primary person who has caused harm being responsible, choosing to be accountable for his or her behavior, admitting any wrong that was done. Taking responsibility also includes a willingness to give an explanation of the harmful behavior. Ideally, this accountability then extends to everyone, as all persons in the Circle deeply search their hearts and minds to discover if there is any part of the matter at hand for which they have some responsibility.

> **RJ rests on the primary person who has caused harm being responsible, choosing to be accountable for his or her behavior, admitting any wrong that was done. Taking responsibility also includes a willingness to give an explanation of the harmful behavior.**

Everyone needs to accept responsibility for his own behavior, but the restorative process begins with the offender's admission.

Restorative practices rest on firm accountability for behavior within a context of care and respect. Without care and respect being apparent, we are not likely to feel safe enough to tell the truth about our own misdeeds. When blaming and shaming intrude, the safety of the Circle is compromised and offenders are likely to retreat into defensiveness. The tendency is to blame others rather than look at our own contribution to the problem; some folks need help to move beyond that habit, and help is best received when wrapped in sincere care and appreciation of the person. The offender must take responsibility for her behavior to qualify for restorative justice, and in our Circles, after initial introductions, the offender is the first to speak, and she tells the story of the crime. Offenders respond to these prompts: *"Tell us what happened. Tell us what you did and why you did it. What were you thinking about at the time? How do you feel about what you did? What has happened since? Who has been affected by this incident, and how were they harmed?"* A full account is required and is followed by an opportunity for the Circle to ask clarifying questions, not to challenge, but ask questions that enhance understanding.

> **Restorative practices rest on firm accountability for behavior within a context of care and respect.**

It is also important to safeguard the victim by interrupting if the offender starts to blame the victim, even subtly suggesting that the victim contributed to the crime. Revictimization may sound like this: *"If she hadn't put all those pots out near the fence, we wouldn't have kicked them." "He just makes me so mad I want to slap him."* We train our facilitators to intercede if an offender makes this kind of statement when telling the story. This is a shifting of responsibility away from self and that interrupts the forward progress of the Circle.

On the other hand, if the offender gives what appears to be an open and honest telling of the story, we breathe easier knowing that the rest of the process will likely go well. Remember Paul Ekman,[18] the researcher who discovered the universality of nonverbal language among humans throughout the world? The nonverbal and the verbal language of the offender's storytelling have to match to satisfy the Circle's need for honesty and remorse. Victims may have some anger that needs to be heard, but they generally soften when they perceive the offender has "come clean." As you might imagine, if the offender is evasive, blames others, makes excuses and leaves out part of the story, the Circle tends to get surly, and a victim's anger is apt to escalate.

It is interesting that some offenders are good at accepting responsibility in the preconference meeting but seem to freeze or shift to making excuses in the Circle. A skillful facilitator may be able to turn this around and get the storytelling back on track, and sometimes help comes from unexpected places.

I recall a Circle for a young man who had posted some pretty ugly things about a teacher on the Internet. We suspected he was using drugs, and, although he had admitted he made the postings, he was a long way from remorseful. "She had been mean to me and she deserved it," but in the preconference he was quick to add, "But I still shouldn't have done it." Though I had some concerns about him, I decided to hold the Circle in hopes her story would touch him. I had no doubt that he needed to be touched.

His parents and his 10 year-old sister came with him to his Circle. He entered the room with a swagger, sat down, crossed his arms in a defensive posture and looked at the floor. I felt a need to break the ice he had brought into the room, so I began by asking everyone to say why they had come tonight and what they hoped to accomplish. The victim began and said she wanted to feel safe with this student again; others spoke of working out the problem and making things right. We were nearly around the Circle when it was little sister's turn. In a very small, tender voice, she said quite simply, "I just want my brother to have a good life." There was profound silence in the room. Her compassionate hope for her brother melted every heart, even her big brother's. His demeanor softened, and the Circle went well. An agreement was reached, but the boy never finished it, for within a few weeks of the Circle he entered a residential drug treatment program. I still think of that little sister and hope that her wish comes true.

∞§∞

Responsibility Extends to Our Community

In ancient times it was clear that each member of the tribe had a responsibility to contribute to the well being of the whole, and everyone's behavior reflected on his family and his tribe. In the *mapuche* communities of Peru and in other indigenous tribes, if a member of the tribe harmed someone from another tribe, the responsibility to make repair rested with the entire tribe.

Today our closest tribal equivalent is our community, and we are still repairing the harm for our members who offend through our tax dollars by paying the costs associated with vandalism to our parks and other public property. When shoplifting occurs, our merchants must repair the harm, and they may pass the costs along to consumers in the community. Through our police, courts, mental health centers, and in many other ways, we all are still making repair for ones in our tribe who do harm. At Teaching Peace we had a restorative program for teens called Shoplifting Solutions Workshop. It was a two-evening program for teens and their parents. As a part of the process, representative merchants attended a Circle to represent the harm to the community from this crime.

Even our facilitators remarked about how much they learned from hearing the merchants. When we address these problems in a restorative way, young people recognize that they are a part of something bigger, our community, and their behavior is having a negative impact there. A teen offender in the LCJP video, *Circles of Justice*, tells us that through his RJ experience, community was no longer an abstract concept; now it has a face.

∞§∞

Discipline Challenges Schools

As previously stated, in ancient times exile from the tribe was the ultimate penalty and was essentially a death sentence, as survival alone was unlikely. There are many parallels to this concept for today's students who face school expulsion. Once they are expelled from their school tribe, they rarely are successful in reintegrating, and their survival in our society without even a high school education is perilous.

Too often schools "blame the lettuce" for its failure to thrive in their garden. Schools have too many mandates and not enough resources to spend the time and make the emotional investment in students who, for *whatever* reason, are not succeeding. The most common response from school personnel to a request that they use restorative discipline is that it takes too much time. School resources are stretched so thin that it may be no more fair to blame the schools than it is to blame the students. Far too much of our resources is being allocated to fight wars and build and staff prisons while our schools remain under funded. Schools may cling to the punishment paradigm not because they believe in it, but because it is fast and manageable. An assistant principal once told me, "I can suspend 10 students in the time it takes me to sit in one Circle." Sadly, true!

Circles are not fast, and they are not always successful, but they are effective most of the time. They typically last one to three hours, depending on the number of participants, as it takes time for all voices to be heard. Even with resource challenges, I wonder how many discipline actions it takes to equal the time investment in a Circle that not only has the capacity to solve the problem, but also teaches self-responsibility.

It is inspiring to watch teenagers conduct discipline Circles in their schools, and that model reduces demand on staff time and achieves another level of student engagement. I suspect the accountability to peers produces even more positive outcomes given the primacy of the peer group in teen culture. For this model to reap the benefits, it needs to be truly restorative and not just student led. I have witnessed Teen Court and other student-led processes that were extremely punitive. It is imperative that facilitators of any age be grounded in a set of principles and values, such as the 5 R's, well trained, and that cases are monitored and debriefed, with attention given to how each case demonstrated restorative principles and values.

> **It is inspiring to watch teenagers conduct discipline Circles in their schools, and that model reduces demand on staff time and achieves another level of student engagement.**

We have worked with schools where high school student teams took responsibility for facilitating weekly restorative discipline circles at a nearby middle school. One week they would conduct preconference meetings with the involved parties and facilitate a Circle with them and an administrator from the school the following week. It is truly delightful to watch what students can do when they are empowered, trained and supported. There is no shortage of responsibility-taking with this group of students and no tolerance for a lack of accountability in others. We knew from our experience at LCJP that when you facilitate processes based in the 5 R's, you cannot help but integrate them into your life.

The Facilitator's Right Role in the Circle

There is also the matter of responsibility for the RJ practitioner. Facilitators sometimes fret over a case that is pending or one they felt did not go well. In debriefing with them about their concerns, we often discover that they forgot it is not their job to "fix" anything. Facilitators are in the Circle to guide a process, not to determine an outcome. If we do not stay clear on our appropriate relationship to the Circle and with all the parties involved, we are more likely to do harm to the Circle, to ourselves, or both. To be able to sustain over time in a helping endeavor, it serves us well to remember our role in the lives of our clients. It is arrogant to think we know what is best for them, and we will not likely survive in doing the work for very long if we try to carry the weight of offenders' life lessons. That does not mean we cannot feel compassion for them; it just means that we do not have to suffer compassion fatigue, which we surely will if we internalize their problems. We need to do our own work and

> **Facilitators are in the Circle to guide a process, not to determine an outcome.**

leave others to do theirs. If we can guide a Circle process that gives voice to victims, accountability to offenders and engages the community in solving its own problems, we have done a significant thing. It is not our responsibility to fix anyone.

It can be challenging for new facilitators to establish and maintain a right relationship to the Circle. Sometimes persons go through our facilitator training process but are unable or unwilling to refrain from giving direct advice to the Circle, despite being trained explicitly not to give advice or suggestions, as it disempowers the Circle in solving its own problems. Due to the inherent power advantage held by the facilitator, the Circle is likely to defer to the facilitator's ideas rather than finding their own.

In this way we differ from some indigenous models, such as Navajo Peacemaking, where a designated elder leads the restorative process and offers suggestions as to how the issues may be resolved. It is essential to note that in these circumstances, the elder has been selected by the tribe to engage with the Circle in this way. This is different from a facilitator who has not been given such authority by the Circle participants, which is the case in most non-tribal, restorative justice processes.

There Is Responsibility Even If You Did Not Intend Harm

Offenders sometimes talk about their crimes as "just a prank" or an accident, and it appears that in many cases there was no intent to do harm; however, that does not absolve people from responsibility for the outcomes of their actions. This is the most difficult part of the lesson about responsibility — we are responsible for our actions even if we did not intend the outcome. "Remember," we remind them, "restorative justice is not just about you. We have a victim and a community that are hurting from your actions. Who should answer to them?" Most offenders look at the floor at this point, recognizing their responsibility.

In one of the saddest cases I can recall, an offender truly was involved in an accident, a deadly one.

A young woman on her first day back to work after maternity leave made a split second decision in traffic that left a motorcyclist dead. It was the kind of thing that could happen to most of us. The light was turning and she went for it, seeing Don, the cyclist, too late. This case only came to restorative justice because Don's parents were adamant that they wanted it. Their son's life was over, and they saw no point in destroying another life. Don's adult son was very angry and refused to attend the Circle, but his daughter and some other family members agreed to participate. The facilitator was one of our best, a retired family therapist whose training and wealth of experience equipped him well for the job. With help from Don's family, a memorial was set up with pictures of Don and other memorabilia. It was the first thing people saw as they entered the room. It made Don real and brought him to the Circle.

The Circle participants were tense at the start. The family spoke of Don and how he would be remembered. There were many tears all around the Circle. The offender told her story, and when her husband spoke it was clear he was angry. Don's parents expressed the desire that this young mother not be destroyed by this tragedy. An agreement was reached and completed. In the debrief and the feedback forms, everyone agreed it had been a good Circle. Case closed.

Years later, I was at a luncheon. In an introduction round I told my name and that I conducted restorative justice Circles with Teaching Peace. A woman across the room threw her arms in the air. Her face completely changed demeanor, like she'd just seen a ghost. "I did that." She said, "My family was in a restorative justice Circle." And she went on to describe this very circle, and then she told me what I hadn't known. From that time forward, the young woman became a regular participant in their family's holiday events. She brings food and gifts, and honors Don's memory with her presence. She has become a part of their family, and Don's son who was too angry to attend the Circle has since recognized that she wasn't that much older than him, and his heart has softened, too. This may be a case where a victim's family redeemed an offender's life, and, by extension, her child's life as well. The good we do ripples, too.

∞§∞

Personal Responsibility Increases Personal Power

It is never too late to take responsibility for your behavior. In Twelve Step programs, participants are expected to do that very thing and to repair harm no matter how long ago it happened. In 2008 the Australian parliament apologized to the aboriginals who were forcibly taken from their families and put in residential schools. Taking responsibility for your behavior is simply an honorable, authentic, and empowering thing to do.

> **Taking responsibility for your behavior is simply an honorable, authentic, and empowering thing to do.**

∞§∞

TIPS: The Language of Responsibility

* **Watch your words.** As a RJ practitioner, I cringe when I hear phrases like, "I didn't have time to get to that," or other phrases that shift responsibility away from the speaker. In this case, he has made it time's problem when, in fact, it was his time management decision to allocate his 24 hours elsewhere that day. We all have the same 24 hours, and we choose what we do with them. A far more authentic response is, "I had other priorities that took precedence, but I should be able to get to it (fill in the blank.)

104

- **The powerful "but."** "But" is an extraordinarily powerful word. It typically has the effect of negating everything that came before it. "*I love you, but. . .*" leaves the dreaded feeling of the hammer that is about to fall and does not make you feel loved at all. In most cases, the word "and" may be substituted for "but" to join ideas without the negative impact. Try it and just notice how rarely you'll find the need to use "but."

- **Use responsible language.** Another way we frequently avoid responsibility is with phrases like, "I couldn't," or "I wasn't able to," when the more honest statement is that we made a different choice. "I couldn't go to his game," could be more responsibly stated, "I had a work priority at the same time as his game." Generally speaking, we choose the things we do. Granted, those choices are heavily influenced by our regard for others or concern for the consequences of not doing them; however, it is still our choice. To frame it as otherwise is abdicating responsibility for our life choices. It frames us as the victim of circumstances rather than the author of our life story. A steady diet of that disempowers the speaker and models a lack of self-responsibility.

- **A taste or a mouthful?** When we take responsibility for something, we need to assess the actual measure we should rightly own. Most times a person is responsible for some part of what has happened, but maybe not all of it. If you say, "I did this, but not that," you invite other people to consider if there is some part of the problem where they may have some responsibility. Be cautious that this strategy is not used to slide around fully owning the responsibility that is rightly yours.

Chapter 8

Why the Restorative Justice Movement is Spreading

In every community there is work to be done. In every nation, there are wounds to heal. In every heart there is the power to do it.

— Marianne Williamson

It makes me quiver to hear someone say, "Oh, yeah, I know what restorative justice is." It is a paradox of knowing; on the one hand, I want people to know what restorative justice is; yet, on the other hand, I'm not sure we ever can fully know. Often, it seems, a cursory exposure to restorative justice registers falsely as full knowing.

Fifteen years of "doing" RJ, and I am still learning, and it is still evolving. In the elegant simplicity of restorative justice, there is a complexity that continues to reveal itself. RJ may be used in a seemingly endless number of applications to prevent conflicts, to resolve problems, to heal wounds at home, in school, at work, at the park, anywhere. The list could go on for pages and

> **In the elegant simplicity of restorative justice, there is a complexity that continues to reveal itself.**

pages and pages, and that's because it is based on principles and values. People sometimes experience or hear about one restorative practice and they think they know what RJ is when, in fact, they have only understood through the hands of one of the blind men who thinks he grasped the whole elephant.

Restorative justice is infinitely simple—just apply the principles—but that does not mean it is easy. Living a life of integrity takes mindfulness, courage and commitment. Restorative justice is something to be lived. It makes my life both simple and rich at the same time, as it provides a reminder of what matters most in life and a guide for my actions. It gives me a theology without a religious affiliation.

> **Living a life of integrity takes mindfulness, courage and commitment. Restorative justice is something to be lived.**

When we live by the 5 R's, many of life's conflicts are prevented. The 5 R's remind us to value relationships and to treat both self and others with respect. They show us how to deal with challenges when they appear with respectful listening, responsibility taking and repair. They teach us about the significance of softening our hearts toward forgiveness so that reintegration may fulfill its magic and bring our path to the high road. *Restorative justice is being embraced all over the world, because it feels exactly right.*

Consistent, Positive Results Across Cultures

At international restorative justice conferences, I have heard people speak from various parts of the world who are implementing restorative practices. They come from England, Ireland, France, Belgium, Australia, New Zealand, Japan, Indonesia, Thailand, Spain, Peru, Bolivia, Chile, Mexico, Caribbean Islands, Canada, Sweden, Newfoundland, numerous states in the U. S., to name a few. When they tell about the outcomes of their programs, they sound very much alike; about 90% of the time it works, and satisfaction ratings are in the high 90 percentages. What system of justice can best those outcomes? *Restorative justice is being embraced all over the world, because it works.*

∞§∞

Restorative Justice Is By and For Communities

Restorative justice is based in a community approach and does not require professionals to deliver it. There are clearly professional gatekeepers — police chiefs, district attorneys, judges, state and city officials, school boards and administrators, whose endorsement and support are required. However, many formal RJ programs rely heavily on volunteers to conduct the restorative practices. This service delivery model is prevalent in Colorado. Teaching Peace organized a coalition of neighboring RJ programs to create the Restorative Justice Training Collaboration that cooperatively provides awareness trainings for schools, and trains community volunteers and school personnel to facilitate Circles. Precious staff time is used to provide training and support for the volunteers who actually deliver the services. This model has the added benefit of promoting strong civic engagement, while we leverage our tight budget dollars to give far more service delivery than could ever be provided by staff alone. *Restorative justice is being embraced all over the world, because it is cost effective.*

∞§∞

Models Evolve While the Principles Remain

Our program started out using one restorative model, the community group conference, which is predicated on there being a victim and an offender. We soon encountered circumstances, especially school-related cases that simply did not fit those role designations. We came to refer to those as mutual responsibility cases where both parties had responsibility for harm done to the other, or cases involving "victimless crimes," like substance abuse or underage alcohol use. We adapted our process and called it a restorative circle.

We also adapted the model to create a workshop approach for shoplifting. Next, we collaborated with a nonprofit that specialized in addressing substance abuse, *Employee and Family Resources* of Des Moines, Iowa, to create a restorative model for use with minors in possession of alcohol called ReThinking Drinking. When you are emphatically clear about your principles and values, it is possible to create new processes that are truly restorative and responsive to the demands of different situations.

Although the restorative ideal is accountability for the offender, voice for the victim, engagement for the community, and repair for all, sometimes we cannot always accomplish all of those. Sometimes the best we can do may be for the community to address the needs of the victim. Community members may hold a healing circle for a victim when the offender is unknown or simply not present for a host of reasons, including the victim's request. Healing occurs when your community gathers around you, bears witness to your story and offers comfort and support to repair the harm you have experienced. There can be miraculous power in having your story heard. Bernie Glassman tells of such experiences leading groups to Holocaust sites in his exquisite book, *Bearing Witness*.

When my community experienced heart-wrenching pain, Teaching Peace hosted a Community Healing Circle.

Community Healing
As told by Linda Leary and Beverly Title

Two young Latinos left another to bleed to death in the street with a sword in his heart, just outside a day care center. The community

110

was horrified and in shock, wondering what to do. The police held a community meeting to share information and give people an opportunity to get involved with community projects involving our youth. It felt like something more was needed, something that went more to the aching hearts. Teaching Peace called a Community Healing Circle, and asked their restorative justice volunteers to facilitate circles in English and Spanish. It was clear that something had to be done or the community would continue to become more fragmented from the pain and fear resulting from a recent gang homicide. We didn't know what kind of turnout we would have as we'd not done this before.

People came, tentative at first, their faces expressing a gamut of emotions, some wounded with fear and sadness, others just cautious. There were Anglo and Latino community members, some with children in tow, representatives from the city, youth agencies, the police, a representative of GRIP (Gang Response and Intervention Program), clergy, community activists—anyone who was concerned enough about the health and safety of the community to come and listen and share their thoughts and ideas.

After introductions and a statement of purpose, the larger Circle reconvened into smaller, more intimate Circles, each with an RJ facilitator. As the poignant stories emerged, it became evident that the people wanted and were determined to find a better way to move forward together, because it was not only impossible but just too frightening to do it alone. The larger Circle re-formed to hear stories from each small Circle.

- *A Hispanic mother who worked two jobs expressed her fear of leaving her 12 year-old daughter alone so much and did not want her out and about in her neighborhood. After fleeing Mexico many years before to escape domestic abuse, she came here hoping for a new life within the safety of what*

111

she called the *"American Dream."* She lamented missing too much of her daughter's life as she worked multiple jobs to provide their livelihood.

- Two sisters talked about how gangs almost destroyed their family, because one of them had been a gang member. She spoke about the courage it took to leave the gang, because it seemed, on the surface, a place in which to belong and feel important and powerful until the violence scared her. When she became pregnant, she saw that this was not what she wanted for her baby and felt fortunate she could return to her family.

- A young Anglo man, who had witnessed political violence in Central America, expressed concern about there being a similar culture of violence right in his own community.

- Three teen siblings expressed concern about the difficulty of staying out of gangs, especially when their friends were joining.

- Some Latinos shared a deep resentment that their culture was being judged and associated with gangs and violence. They didn't want the Anglos to believe that, and, more importantly, they didn't want their children to.

- Another mother living within the Hispanic neighborhood was so fearful that she would not allow her children to play in their own backyard because of the presence of gangs.

- A man who had spent time in prison came with his teenage son and his son's friend. He had big hopes for his son having a different kind of life. The son wore a mask of boredom.

112

Who knows what he heard that night, but he couldn't miss the message that his father cared.

The sharing of stories could have gone on well into the night. Once people realized they were among interested listeners and it was safe to speak, the floodgates opened. One teen girl even asked if she could come back the following week and continue. Our community didn't solve its gang problem that night, but people made new connections and felt that their neighbors better understood their burdens, their fears, their hopes, and most importantly, that others cared.

∞§∞

In this story we see another face of justice, one that can address the collective pain of a community. Is that not also an important function of justice?

Community comes together on a number of levels. There is another community that develops for us; it is the community that forms among restorative justice practitioners. I can go into a community anywhere in the world and if there is an RJ program, I have friends, folks who speak the same language, live by the same values, recognize the importance of relationship and have an unusual capacity for sitting and listening. Teaching Peace and the LCJP are just one of many shining examples.

> **Like the sorcerers of old, the Circle produces the alchemy to transform base experience into golden wisdom and compassion.**

Each program may look a bit different, as there is not one right way to do restorative practices.

Many models are evolving and sometimes they are known by different names, such as community group conference, restorative circle, peacemaking circle, healing circle. And some are crime specific, such as ReThinking Drinking and Shoplifting Solutions

Workshops. Some people call RJ Justice that Heals or Transformational Justice. Like the sorcerers of old, the Circle produces the alchemy to transform base experience into golden wisdom and compassion. A rose by any other name . . . *Restorative justice is being embraced all over the world, because it is dynamic, robust and adaptable to meet our needs.*

∞§∞

A Community of Friends

In his book, *Peace is Every Step*, within a chapter called "Investing in Friends," Nobel Peace Prize winner Thich Nhat Hanh writes:

Even if we have a lot of money in the bank, we can die very easily from our suffering. So, investing in a friend, making a friend into a real friend, building a community of friends, is a much better source of security. We will have someone to lean on, to come to, during our difficult moments.

We can get in touch with the refreshing, healing elements within and around us thanks to the loving support of other people. If we have a good community of friends, we are very fortunate. To create a good community, we first have to transform ourselves into a good element in the community. After that, we can go to another person and help him or her become an element of the community. We build our network of friends that way. We have to think of friends and community as investments, as our most important asset. They can comfort us and help us in difficult times, and they can share our joy and happiness.[19]

With the practice of restorative justice we are constantly in the process of building communities of friends. We build enduring friends among fellow practitioners. We facilitate the repair of relationships and strengthen bonds among Circle participants in virtually every Circle we convene. A stronger community emerges when citizens regularly engage in Circles and embrace other community members who are struggling to regain wholeness following a conflict or criminal event in their lives. I have witnessed relationships in workplaces move from hostility to support from the experience of a Circle. And I have seen people who work in criminal justice organizations become more positively connected to their work and to their colleagues through the implementation of restorative justice in their workplace. *Restorative justice is being embraced all over the world, because of its power to build and rebuild communities of friends.*

> **A stronger community emerges when citizens regularly engage in Circles and embrace other community members who are struggling to regain wholeness following a conflict or criminal event in their lives.**

∞§∞

RJ Moves Beyond Criminal Justice

RJ is adaptable to accommodate many programmatic needs, and it is also robust in its application within various institutions. Professionals in criminal justice, patrol officers, school resource officers, court administrators, judges, probation officers, victim services specialists, and a host of others have experienced a sense of professional renewal through the introduction of restorative practices in their workplaces. For the past 15 years, I have had many opportunities to interface with them, and it is inspiring to see that many of them have embraced restorative practices and received a professional "new lease on life."

I have seen numerous education professionals — superintendents, principals, assistant principals, teachers, counselors, coaches, specialists, directors, interventionists, school psychologists, paraprofessionals, campus supervisors — enlivened by and passionate about using restorative practices. Many of them attend our training and stay in touch, sharing their experiences of using Circles in their classrooms, offices, hallways, playgrounds and auditoriums. A RJ colleague was just hired to be the Dean of School Culture at a local charter school that is focused on becoming a "restorative school." A superintendent at a nearby school district spoke to the district staff saying they were going to administer discipline by forming relationships with students and the way they were going to do that was with restorative discipline. Teaching Peace is currently collaborating with our local school district to provide an application called RATES (Restorative Alternative to School Expulsion and Suspension.)

Universities are using restorative practices to manage problems in dorms and in judicial affairs. The University of Colorado in Boulder collaborates with the City of Boulder Municipal Court to address virtually all alcohol offenses through an on-campus RJ program. David Karp and Thom Allena[20] wrote about applications of RJ at the university level in *Restorative Justice on the College Campus: Promoting Student Growth and Responsibility, and Reawakening the Spirit of Campus Community.*

Governmental entities are also finding that restorative practices can successfully replace some of their tired ways of addressing

Governmental entities are also finding that restorative practices can successfully replace some of their tired ways of addressing wearisome problems.

116

wearisome problems. A colleague and I did a "restorative intervention" for a city department that led to resolution of some major personnel and morale problems that had been going on for a long time. Restorative justice programs are relieving overcrowded court dockets and in some places community accountability boards (CABs) are carrying out probation monitoring and more.

Social Service institutions are using a model called Family Group Decision Making with issues of child welfare. They bring together people who know the child, close and extended family members, friends, perhaps teachers and others, to figure out what is in the very best interest of this child, as opposed to those decisions being made by professionals and judges who have little or no personal relationship with the child.

And let's not overlook the institution of the family. A single mother who worked with us adapted the restorative approach to create a parenting process that worked for her. When her boys "got into it," she would send them to their rooms with instruction not to come out until they could say what they had done that hurt their brother and give a good apology. Over the years, many parents who participated in our Circles because their children were offenders reported that they learned from RJ how to hold their kids accountable while still being loving towards them. They learned from the experience of firm accountability within a context of care.

I have been privileged to interface with people in all of these arenas, and it is wonderful to see how awakened they become with the introduction of restorative practices in their fields. *Restorative justice is being embraced all over the world, because it has capacity to assist renewal of our institutions.*

117

RJ Provides a Moral Compass

Teachers, especially middle class teachers of European descent like me, often lament the fact that kids come to school without a common set of values and norms. It makes our job harder when one child has been taught at home never to hit, while another's parents support hitting as acceptable if someone is being aggressive toward you.

As our society has become increasingly multicultural, multilingual, and multiethnic, it rests with the schools to establish common values and norms. Yet in the values clarification era of the 70's and 80's, we saw teachers losing their jobs for "teaching values." Today we are recognizing that schools must have a set of principles and values that everyone is expected to honor, but we've relabeled the concept. Now it is called mission statement or vision, maybe even principles and values, and we endorse curricula that address conflict resolution, bullying prevention, social responsibility, social and emotional learning, just to name a few. Lane Lasater 's work on social responsibility is impressive, as is the work of Rachael Kessler with the PassageWorks Institute. Her book, *The Soul of Education*, recognizes what school psychologist Art Combs asserted, that children cannot learn in a valueless classroom. In homogeneous communities, we used to rely on the church, or the shaman, to establish these values, but today many people do not participate in organized religions. Our society is crying out for a set of values and principles we can all embrace that are not based in religious doctrine. The 5 R's offer precisely that. *Restorative justice is being embraced all over the world, because it provides a moral compass.*

RJ Reveals our Collective Intelligence

People want to be heard. Most crime victims we talk to want a voice in the process, as do most police officers, neighbors, friends and family. In our criminal justice system, voices of victims and community (witnesses) are silenced or filtered, as they are only allowed to answer questions posed by attorneys or a judge, *if they are present at all*. Offenders do not have to speak for themselves; in fact, their attorneys have likely instructed them not to speak.

When I was in my 20's I had the experience of being a witness in a trial. I was stunned by the fact I was not allowed to tell the story of what happened. I could only answer questions put to me by the attorneys or the judge, and my experience was that those answers added up to a slanted perspective, not really giving the whole story. Had I been asked, which I was not, I would have rated the experience as low as possible on a satisfaction scale — far from the 95% or higher ratings restorative justice typically receives from *all* participant groups.

RJ is democracy in action: participatory democracy. In the RJ process there is ample opportunity for community members to be directly involved in addressing a major community problem, crime. Whether one facilitates the Circle or sits as a representative of the community voice, she is bringing

> **RJ is democracy in action: participatory democracy.**

community to life. I had the privilege of hearing John Braithwaite,[21] criminal justice scholar and RJ advocate from New Zealand, speak at a conference in Veldhoven, the Netherlands. He suggested if institutional authority and social order is interrupted, through acts of God, accident or terrorism, communities that have RJ will be prepared; they will have a mechanism to come together, address their problems and find solutions that re-establish civil society. As remote as that might sound, according to *The Walking People*,[22] it was precisely what inspired the crossing of the Bering Straits and the development of Native American council process of governance, which is more of a sibling than a cousin to RJ. In that brilliant and beautiful tome, *The Walking People,* Paula Underwood, whose Tribal name was Turtle Woman Singing, tells of the tsunami that swept away all the tribal leaders and inspired a form of governance that rests with all the people, so never again would the tribe find themselves leaderless.

RJ also addresses our yearning for community, to feel closeness, connectedness, and intimacy with others, especially with those who live nearby. RJ requires that we open our hearts to each other and tell our truth. You may be surprised how easy that becomes when one person starts the ball rolling. It is the kind of justice that has the power of community, the power to heal our souls. *Restorative justice is being embraced all over the world, because it brings us back to each other.*

∞§∞

RJ Supports our Humanity

Remember the father whose son was victim of the playground "pile driver" that left him seriously injured? Remember his compassion for the young offender? Remember the RJ facilitator who worked for years helping the female gang members discover a better way? Remember the young man who sprayed slush on the pedestrians? Remember the relationship he developed with the injured Captain that opened his eyes and his heart? RJ practitioners carry hundreds of stories like these in their hearts. The more we sit

> **The more we sit in the sacred Circle together, the more our humanity is increased.**

in the sacred Circle together, the more our humanity is increased. *Restorative justice is being embraced all over the world, because it leads us to be better human beings.*

∞§∞

Restorative Justice Offers Hope for our Planet

The collapse of the global economy, deforestation of the rain forests, the ugly rise of terrorism around the globe — all these and more are leading many to believe we have gone too far. Dominance, greed and gluttony have ruled and have brought us to the brink of destruction.

The optimists among us envision reducing the dominance, greed and gluttony with a new set of values to guide us — like responsibility, empathy and sustainability. Barbara Marx Hubbard

> **The optimists among us envision reducing the dominance, greed and gluttony with a new set of values to guide us — like responsibility, empathy and sustainability.**

puts forward the concept of conscious evolution that she describes as a new social/scientific/spiritual meta-discipline that aims to find solutions to today's problems. We are part of an ever-expanding consciousness, and we are all evolving, whether we want to or not. "At this time of rapid change in human society and global ecology there is a need for the connecting, coordinating and integrating of individual and organizational initiatives working on behalf of balanced, ethical and life-enhancing evolution for humanity and Earth." [23]

In recent conversation, Barbara Marx Hubbard recognized restorative justice as one such solution that is assisting our social evolution. I am encouraged by people like her with the wisdom to envision a better world and the heart to settle for nothing less. And there are many wonderful people working on amazing solutions. The *One Voice* project brings moderate Israelis and Palestinians together in a search for solutions to their costly conflict. Restorative justice is also at work in Northern Ireland.

> **We are part of an ever-expanding consciousness, and we are all evolving, whether we want to or not.**

Restorative justice is being embraced all over the world, because it may just save our planet.

Chapter 9
Repair - The Fourth R

Tuntuam was waiting for us inside in the traditional manner of a kakaram warrior. He sat on a stool in the center of his home, before a blazing fire. In one hand he held a spear and in the other a single-shot, muzzle-loaded rifle, a prized gift from a man who had once insulted him and had presented him with this weapon in order to win clemency — and save his life.

—John Perkins, *Spirit of the Shuar*

The act of repairing harm done to another is perhaps as old as time itself. The restorative approach requires that the harm be repaired to the greatest extent possible, recognizing that some harm may be beyond anyone's capacity to fully repair. It is the principle of repair that allows injured persons to set aside thoughts of revenge and punishment. Once the persons who caused harm have accepted responsibility for their behavior, they hear from others how they were harmed by their action. Even if the offender did not intend the harm, it is her responsibility to make repair. It is through taking responsibility for one's own behavior and making repair that offenders may regain or strengthen their self-respect. Quite simply, it is the honorable thing to do.

> **It is through taking responsibility for one's own behavior and making repair that offenders may regain or strengthen their self-respect.**

∞§∞

Even If You Did Not Intend Harm

Some teens balk at the idea that they are responsible for repair if they did not mean harm. I tell them this true story.

One very hot day, I stopped in a coffee shop to get a cool drink. They were having a special on a whipped blueberry drink, and I love blueberries. Walking back to my car, my heel caught on the curb; I tripped and threw that drink all over someone's car. Yikes! I lost my drink and made a mess. I looked around and saw no one. I could have probably gotten away with just driving off, but as a restorative justice practitioner, I knew I had responsibility, and I needed to make repair. So I went to my car, got out some paper and wrote an apology note. Fortunately, that day I had some cash in my wallet, so I put it in the note saying, "I'm so sorry that my accident made a mess of your car. And I apologize for your inconvenience of cleaning it up. Please accept my apology, and get a car wash on me." It wasn't a perfect solution, but it was the best I could think to do. So imagine this was your car. How would you feel when you walked up and saw the mess? How would you feel when you opened the door and found the note I had slid through the crack in your window. What kind of community do you want to live in?

Collectively, the Circle Determines Repair

We ask offenders to make repair to their victim, to their community, to themselves and their family. In every case what is appropriate to accomplish the repair is from the perspective of the persons harmed or their representative, as in the case of the community repair. Offenders are expected to take direct action to accomplish the repair, and they, too, have a voice in deciding.

The facilitator suggests to the Circle that coming up with the repair ideas be seen as a challenge to their creativity. How can this young person's assets, that the Circle just reviewed, be used to accomplish the needed repair? After everyone speaks to what they would like to have the offender do to make repair, it will get pared down to a formal, written agreement of three to five items. The next step in getting to the agreement is to ask the offender, "After hearing all these ideas from the Circle, what will you do to make things right?" We listen carefully as the offender "self sentences." I believe the self-sentence, the offender actively making these choices, contributes significantly to our 90% agreement completion rates.

After she tells what she will do to repair the harm, the Circle is asked if that satisfies them. If not, the facilitator helps participants negotiate the final agreement, leading the Circle in the tough work of determining how much is enough and what is too much. In Olmert's book, she discusses mirror neurons in our brains which allow us to "resonate with the thoughts, intentions, and feelings of others. . . they allow us to grasp the minds of others. . .by feeling, not thinking."[24] It is typical that Circles seem to have this capacity to easily come to agreement, and this is especially true when the members are satisfied that the offender has taken responsibility and demonstrated so by offering to make repair.

A final date is set when all items must be completed or the case will be referred back to the police. The agreement is tested to make sure it is a good agreement. Good agreements are measurable, in that each item may be tracked, and we can know that it has been completed; achievable, all items are within the offender's ability to complete; and they must fit the offense, not having generic items.

Sometimes it is helpful to frame the offender's repair of harm to herself in terms of what will help her recognize different options, ones that do not cause harm, the next time she is in a similar situation. Once details of the agreement are finalized, the facilitator congratulates the Circle on their good work and invites them to have some refreshments, sometimes referred to as Breaking Bread, while the final agreement is written up, and everyone signs it before leaving. It always serves to put agreements in writing and sign them, even informal ones among family members or school children. Later, memory of the agreement may not be the same for all parties.

Sample agreement items:

- *A teenage girl who shoplifted because she wanted a new summer wardrobe returned the clothes with tags and unworn after her parents discovered them. She worked to earn twice the value of the items stolen that she used to take homeless shelter children shopping for new school clothes in the fall.*

- *A teen artist made posters with images that appeal to his age group with anti-violence messages. These were displayed in his school.*

- *A boy wrote a song about the negative impact of bullying that contained all the elements of an apology and played it for his victim.*

- *Students sometimes research a topic related to their offense and write an article that they submit for publication to their school newspaper. They are given the option of submitting with or without their name being given, to avoid public shaming.*

- *When teens do things that make all teens suspect, like shoplifting, they often use their talents in a public forum to make teens look good. This may involve the use of an artistic talent, or a gift for academics or an ability to work well with young children. The service they perform may be an artistic product (like a poster) or performance (like a theatre piece) or mentoring younger students at school, babysitting at a community meeting, organizing games for children at a neighborhood block party, teaching their own sibling a new skill, like skateboarding, or tutoring other students.*

- *Circles frequently advocate for public speaking, but we rarely allow that item into a contract. Though it seems like a good idea, our experience shows that it is rarely successful or helpful, and the inherent potential for shaming may do far more harm than good.*

Each agreement is unique to the Circle that creates it. Generally, one or more written apologies are included, though some people prefer face-to-face, spoken apologies. If there is financial loss associated with the crime, restitution is usually expected; however, a victim may not really care about the money and have other wishes for repair. Community service is fairly

> **Each agreement is unique to the Circle that creates it.**

often included, and it must be specifically tailored to the harm that was done and not punitive in nature. Picking up trash on the highway, for example, would not be acceptable unless the offender had littered a highway. Educational activities, like researching a topic, attending an AA meeting, making dinner for the family, taking an anger management class, interviewing an elder, improving school attendance or performance, are highly effective agreement items. In fact, LCJP's evaluation showed that educational items correlate strongly with successful program completion.

127

It is important to double check that none of the items feel punitive; they should truly be designed to move the person gently to a next step of understanding. That does not mean that they cannot be hard, just not that they feel *intended* to hurt. There must be a sense of reciprocity and fairness for the offender to be restored which reduces the likelihood of recidivism.

When a person takes responsibility, clearly recognizes the impact of their deed and shows remorse, a great deal is repaired in the Circle itself. In very rare cases all the work is completed in the Circle, and no one wants anything more. More often, very creative reparations bring deep satisfaction to victims and great learning to offenders that help them remember to make different decisions the next time they are confronted with an opportunity for wrongdoing.

> **There must be a sense of reciprocity and fairness for the offender to be restored which reduces the likelihood of recidivism.**

While we expect it of offenders, some victims actually see *the benefits to the offender* as balancing out what happened to them (the victims) and are grateful for the opportunity to benefit that person in this way. I regularly encounter big-hearted people with this work, and I often say the best part of my work is the people it brings to my life! Role models of compassion and empathy, our higher emotions, regularly show up in our Circles.

∞§∞

Bringing the Lessons Home

Repair agreements vary widely. The victims and community members, not facilitators or program staff, determine what is needed. We specifically train our facilitators not to offer suggestions but to stay focused on conducting the process and leave the content to the Circle. Sometimes, especially in cases with young children, the Circle assists the offender to figure out how they will accomplish the repair. This young offender learned a valuable lesson about personal property, the victim's and his, at a very young age.

> *Dear Johnsons,*
>
> *I didn't like selling my stuff but I deserved it. I shouldn't have stolen your stuff otherwise I wouldn't have to sell my stuff. I was hurt to hear my mom say after I said, can I play my Nintendo, and then my mom said, we sold it.*
>
> *I am sorry for stealing your stuff. In stead of going in your camper I should of knocked on your door and told you that your camper door was unlocked. But in stead I made a choice to steal from your camper. I am sorry for taking the knives, compass, and etc. I don't think I will ever do this again.*
>
> *Sincerely,*
>
> *Andy (9 years old)*

∞§∞

A Good Apology Is Powerful

Most often victims want an apology, but a frivolous apology actually exacerbates rather than repairs harm. We seem to all be taught that apology equals saying you are sorry, and it appears to have been accepted practice for many to toss out a "sorry" while on the run. Apologies need to be sincere, take responsibility for the behavior, name the harm that was done, show remorse for that harm, and, ideally, contain a promise not to do it again. We have created some guidelines for what makes a good apology (see Appendix 3) that are given to offenders when they have this item in their agreement. Our program staff always reviews apologies before they are delivered to victims to guard against re-victimization.

Sometimes items are suggested and selected by the offender for the agreement that are important to the repair, but they are not measurable. An item cannot go in the agreement if it is not measurable, so we devised a way to honor the request and get the offender's assent. We call them "Good Faith Agreements." The facilitator explains why the item cannot go into the agreement, but suggests that the offender can make a promise in front of this Circle about it, and that we believe he is honorable and will be good to his word about it. Sometimes I ritualize it further by asking the two parties involved if they are willing to shake on it, in which case I ask them to stand and shake hands, after the offender states what he will do. These items may be the most important of all to the victim.

I won't spread rumors about you again, and I will tell my friends not to either.

I promise to speak up or tell a teacher the next time I see someone bullying you.

I won't give you dirty looks anymore.

∞§∞

Subtle and Profound Communication

Misinterpreting someone's words or nonverbal communication can compromise the repair process. When we interpret others' actions, it is wise to recognize cultural norms. Remember, again, Paul Ekman's research showing that people all over the world interpret facial grimaces in the same way?

Eye contact and handshakes are related to this nonverbal communication, and they vary among cultures. In Anglo society, direct eye contact is associated with honesty. I can still hear my mother's reprimand when she thought I was being less than truthful, *"Look me in the eye, Little Girl, when you speak to me."* However, Native Americans and many other cultures consider direct eye contact aggressive, a sign of disrespect. There are similar differences among cultures related to how we shake hands. Anglos are taught to give a firm handshake and look people in the eye when we meet them. Traditional Latinos, and others, offer you a gentle hand to shake, thereby suggesting courtesy, respect, a lack of hostility.

Quoting from *Dancing with a Ghost: exploring Indian reality* by Rupert Ross, one of my favorite RJ books:

> *I had just finished a court session on a remote reserve, one in which a community Elder had again been of invaluable assistance by advising the court on appropriate sentences for each offender. I had gone up to him, looked him straight in the eye, shook his hand and told him, in effusive terms, how much I appreciated his contribution. I learned from Charlie that I had made two basic errors.*

> *First, he advised, verbal expressions of praise and gratitude are embarrassing and impolite, especially in the presence of others. The proper course is to quietly ask the person to continue making his contribution next time around.*

> *Second, looking someone straight in the eye, at least among older people in that community, was a rude thing to do. It sends a signal that you consider that person in some fashion inferior. The proper way to send a signal of respect was to look down or to the side, with only occasional glances up to indicate attention. I had been trying to say one thing but had*

131

done so in a way which conveyed exactly the opposite. To my great relief, Charlie also assured me that the man had probably not taken offence; he knew, after all, that a great many white men simply hadn't learned how to behave in a civilized fashion! [25]

∞§∞

Repair within Families

Sometimes I leave a Circle with the feeling that the most significant accomplishment was repairing of relations within the offender's family. The offender's mother is often the first to cry and his father the first to make apology. Though it can happen to any parents, if a child is apprehended by the police, his parents often

> **Though it can happen to any parents, if a child is apprehended by the police, his parents often experience a sense of personal failure. It is as if we failed in our prime directive to raise our children well.**

experience a sense of personal failure. It is as if we failed in our prime directive to raise our children well. If the parent dredges up some parenting task left unattended or incomplete — and who of us can 't think of a few of those — then the sense of failure is even greater. There are also cultural norms that may dictate responsibility for the parents to make amends to the victim's family. We had a traditional Latino family who had been forbidden by the school to have any contact with the victim's family. When they entered the Circle, the first thing on their minds was to make apology, father to father. Relations within those families are disturbed until that obligation can be fulfilled.

It is also common for the connections among family members to be disturbed. Some families try to protect younger siblings and

132

grandparents by concealing what has happened. One of the saddest, most impactful moments I have experienced was when an adult daughter told her sixty-five year old mother who had embezzled thousands of dollars, "I don't know what to tell my son about Grandma." The collective heart of that whole Circle sank with those words.

I encourage families to include siblings in the Circle who are mature enough to respect the process; clearly babies and toddlers cannot participate appropriately, and the suitable age varies with the child. I have seen six year-olds do well, and others of that age would disrupt the Circle's work. In most cases, it is better for them to witness the process than to create their own version of "what's going on with my sister." Sometimes they make excellent contributions, like the little girl who wanted her brother to have a good life. They may also offer good insight on what a sibling can and cannot do — what's enough and what's too much.

A teenager had an agreement item to take his younger brother to the park and teach him how to skateboard. He brought pictures of the little guy skateboarding to our office to validate his completion of that item.

Families may also need repair of their relationships to each other. A common theme among parents of teens is concern that the youth has withdrawn from the family and the repair needed is about re-establishing communication. Finding ways to reconnect them can lead to wonderful agreement items.

As a part of his agreement, a teenager was to drive his mom each Saturday to do her errands, so they could have "windshield time" together and discuss his activities. He provided a driving log of destinations and topics discussed to certify completion of this item of his agreement.

Probably the most common and most challenging repair items for families have to do with the harm of broken trust. More than a few times I have heard a parent express that trust has been broken, and once it is gone you just cannot get it back. I shudder, thinking of the times I had to earn back my parent's trust, with gratitude that they did not slam that door shut. Trust is delicate as a gnat; you cannot really move it without damaging it. I could be faithful to an expectation for a hundred days, but if I violated it on day 101, I had to have that respect conversation with my father again. If trust could not be rebuilt, few, if any, of us would still be in relationships. Violating trust is one of the ways we learn where the lines are that cannot be crossed without serious consequence. It can, in fact, help us learn how to more fully respect each other by increasing our understanding of what we hold as most important. For me, honesty was the thing I most prized; for another parent it may be trustworthiness, or kindness, or respect, or any number of other values. Trust can be restored by making a promise, and then being good to your word, about whatever it is that really matters to the other person.

> **If trust could not be rebuilt, few, if any, of us would still be in relationships.**

> **Trust can be restored by making a promise, and then being good to your word, about whatever it is that really matters to the other person.**

A teenage boy did house chores without having to be told; his mother certified that he did.

A young woman would call her parents to make an alternate plan if she was not home by 6:00 for dinner; she kept a log that her mother signed off when that happened and what were the circumstances.

A young mother interviewed her grandmother about what she thought was most important about parenting; she composed a paper of her grandmother's wisdom to share with her mother and to validate completion of the item.

A 15 year-old girl broke a window to gain access to a house for two 17 year-old boys she wanted to impress. For an item in her agreement, she studied up on assertiveness and refusal skills, then created five statements that she carried on a card in her wallet for the next time she needed a way out of a sticky situation, as would surely happen.

∞§∞

TIPS: The Language of Repair

- **Show sensitivity to victims**. Talking about healing and forgiveness with victims is tricky, and it is safest to be cautious in using those words. This is a highly charged topic in the victim services community. Healing comes to different folks in their own time and their own way and it may never come at all. It is not appropriate to tell a victim that they should heal, or get over it, or that it is time to give it up and move on.

- **What to say and not say**. Oddly, it is never a good idea to say, *"I understand how you feel."* Even if the exact thing has happened to you, you may experience it differently than someone else. In fact, it can be infuriating to the victim who is thinking, *"You couldn't possibly know how this feels to me!"* The better approach is to say, *"It's understandable to feel . . ."* and then reflect what

135

they have said. The very best we can do for victims is to listen, reflect and give messages that express empathy, *"I'm so sorry this happened to you."*

- **Ask the other people.** When harm has been done, sometime those who caused the harm feel so contrite that they rush to repair before consulting the people who have been harmed to find out what repair they actually want. If you feel you need to make repair, do not assume you know what another wants. Ask them first, *"What can I do to help make this right?"* They may say they don't know, so it may be useful to have some suggestions in mind before you ask. Your suggestions may just prime the pump and get them to thinking about what would actually help them.

- **Look at the opposite side.** When I am searching for repair items, it helps to look at the harm and then think about what lies on its opposite side. If someone's reputation is harmed, ask, *"What might enhance her social standing?"* If an act has diminished the image of teenagers in the eyes of the community, for example, what project might enhance their image? If something has diminished someone's self esteem, suggest things that might lift it.

- **Sincerity is essential.** Just as an insincere compliment is more insulting than complimentary, the same is true for apology or any other act of repair. If it cannot be done with sincerity and good will, you are not yet ready to do it at all.

- **How much is enough? How much is too much?** Sometimes people who have been victimized want the proverbial pound of flesh in return. Whenever possible, base quantities on real numbers. For example, if mom has taken time off work and given up personal time to deal with this situation, she may want that many hours of chores done for her in return. If a teacher has lost a

136

certain number of hours of planning time to address a rule violation, he may ask for the offender to do an equal number of hours of internet research to find media resources and other ideas for a topic the teacher is going to cover soon in class, which is what his planning time would otherwise have been used for. Make it as real as possible. Arbitrary numbers and tasks are more likely to be punitive than restorative.

- **Listen and reflect.** Most victims want to be heard, and they want an apology. The apology is sweeter if given *after* they've been fully heard. Let her know she has been fully heard by reflecting her words back to her. *"I see that you were frightened by finding me on your porch, and that mattered more to you than the flower pots I broke getting there."* After the person seems to have finished telling their story, ask, *"Is there anything else you'd like to tell me?"* This shows them you are really willing to listen to the whole thing and that may help lead the victim towards healing.

- **Give an apology and make it a good one**. When making apology, include a statement of remorse followed by a clear statement of responsibility, like *"I regret that I. . ."* and tell *exactly* what you did. Show that you heard how they were impacted. *"I heard that it made you feel _____ and _____."* It helps if you can identify what mattered most to them. *"You helped me see the most important part about this for you was. . ."* And finally, give a promise not to do it again and tell what you will do instead. *"I will never bother your home again, and the next time I'm in this situation, I will . . ."*

Chapter 10
The Language of Restorative Justice: The Five R's-- Relationship, Respect, Responsibility, Repair, Reintegration

---

May the warmth of complexity shine on your face.
May the winds of good change blow gently at your back.
May your feet find the roads of authenticity.
May the web of change begin!

—John Paul Lederach,
The Little Book of Conflict Transformation

I came to RJ with a background in conflict resolution, and, after working with RJ for some time, I became interested in how it could be adapted for use in our everyday lives rather than always being about a formal process that is delivered by a program. I was used to Circles that were usually about 6 – 15 people and had designated facilitators. I began to question if a Circle could be two people, or if you could even Circle yourself. As I worked with questions such as these, I discovered most things that applied to the Circle process could be adapted for dealing with another person where there was a conflict, and these same principles could be used to settle an internal conflict.

The voice of the community members would be lost, and when that is significant in intrapersonal or one-to-one circumstances, a respected person could be consulted for insight and balance. It is also important to protect the speaking and listening process, so it remains a sacred process that doesn't degenerate into the back and forth banter of day-to-day conversation. With those two accommodations, the restorative justice approach can help us prevent conflict in our daily life, and, when conflict does occur, resolve it in a way that strengthens our empathy, understanding and relationships in the process.

∞§∞

Verbal and Non-Verbal Language is Powerful

The language we need for communicating and focusing our personal story telling is imbedded in the 5 R's, and it entails verbal and nonverbal, paralinguistic communications. Paralinguistic communications are defined by Olmert as, "The expressive primal sounds and gestures that reveal emotions such as anger, fear, panic, sadness, surprise. . ." [26] In fact, the nonverbal may convey the more trusted messages. We have all likely heard someone say, "Well, it was just the way she said it" to justify their interpretation of the meaning. To do conflict well, we must be authentic in communication so our verbal and non-verbal messages are congruent. Remember Olmert's reference to those mirror neurons in

> **Whether or not we trust what another says has more to do with our intuitive feelings, inspired by their non-verbal language, than what words we hear.**

our brains which allow us to read each others nonverbal cues. [27] Whether or not we trust what another says has more to do with our intuitive feelings, inspired by their non-verbal language, than what words we hear. This is not to imply that the words do not matter, because they do, but if the words are incongruent with the paralinguistic signals, the latter will win.

A Case of Misjudgment

Two teenage boys were shooting Co2 enhanced BB guns from a second floor bedroom window. Their BB's broke out windows in a neighbor's house and car and did other damage. The neighbors were grandparents that kept their grandchildren who normally would have been playing in the yard that day but were at a cousin's house for a play date. The grandparents, a husband and wife, were certain these boys were gang members. One was Latino and dressed "gangster style," according to the wife. When we met them for the preconference, they were so afraid of these boys that the husband wanted to know if we could use metal detectors to secure the room where the Circle would be held. We wouldn't do that, but we would hold the Circle in the Community Room at the Safety and Justice Building, and a police officer would participate in the Circle. They agreed.

The beginning was tense as the boys sauntered in dressed in black and looking a bit intimidating, as 17 year-olds can. They appeared to be listening carefully to the victim's story, and looked up and made eye contact when grandma told about her fear that her grandchildren could no longer safely play in their yard. After she finished, I asked the boys if they had anything they wanted to say. The Latino boy looked at the couple and gave a spontaneous, heartfelt apology, "I am so sorry. I take care of my little sisters a lot, and I would never want them to get hurt. I would never do anything to hurt your grandkids."

The Circle progressed easily from then on, as all tension dissipated with his words. It was revealed that neither of the boys had fathers living in their homes. My practice at the end of the Circle is to select someone to have the last word — an act of power in our culture —

141

and that night I chose the grandfather. He took his time before speaking, and then said, "A lot has been said here tonight, and I understand that you boys are growing up without your dads. I've raised five boys, and they've come up pretty good. I know that sometimes a boy just needs to talk to a man. If you find yourself needing that, you just come and knock on my door."

When people complain about Circles taking too long, I often think of this Circle. How long would it take to move from being afraid to enter the same room with someone to inviting him to knock on your door? Two hours seems a short time for such a long walk.

∞§∞

Putting the 5 R's to Work in Our Everyday Lives

Let's return for a moment to revisit Howard Zehr's definition of restorative justice from Chapter 6, and take a little liberty with it to see how it may apply beyond the criminal justice system. "Conflict ~~Crime~~ is a violation of people and relationships. It creates obligations to make things right. Resolution ~~Justice~~ involves the affected parties ~~the victim, the offender, and the community~~ in a search for solutions which promote repair, reconciliation, and reassurance." Now instead of an approach to addressing crime, it becomes a conflict resolution process that puts the emphasis on restoring both individuals and damaged relationships. My graduate studies of conflict resolution focused on solving the problem, when, it now

My graduate studies of conflict resolution focused on solving the problem, when, it now seems to me, the primary work is better focused on healing relationships of the parties involved.

142

seems to me, the primary work is better focused on healing relationships of the parties involved. Of course, these two purposes may overlap, but in the restorative approach, the latter becomes the priority.

When we adopt this framework of viewing conflict, it is no longer about who is right or wrong, and "doing conflict" is not about defending behavior. It becomes about how people have been violated and what *they* need to make it right, which may be as simple as an apology. I have been in Circle with crime victims who refuse financial restitution though they had monetary losses; instead they wanted the offender to do well in school, to get involved with positive social activities, to engage actively with his family.

When there is a conflict to resolve or a need for discipline at school or home, the language of restorative justice can serve you well. Our society is averse to engaging in conflict because of fear, trauma, lack of skill and lack of trust. We need a safe framework that is simple enough for us all to know we can navigate successfully. In the face of potential conflict, most people either explode in anger or silently depart, and both strategies may result in sacrifice of important relationships. While we may have to dig deep and bring up things that we've kept hidden, perhaps even masked from ourselves, the 5 R's give us a way to do that and reduce the pain since it is done with respect and in a context of care.

The restorative way to approach conflict is contained in the 5 R's:

- **Relationship and Respect** – These are values and behaviors we carry into the process.
- **Responsibility** – This R speaks to our ability to listen to another's story and fully tell our own story with complete honesty.

- **Repair** – We agree to repair the harm we caused to the extent possible, even if we didn't intend the harm.
- **Reintegration** – This R requires a willingness to open our heart's door to let another back in once they have demonstrated their integrity by accepting responsibility and repairing the harm to the extent possible.

Conflict doesn't have to be brutal, leaving people feeling beat up and hurt. It can be worked through in a way that solves the immediate problem and restores or builds positive relationships for the future among the people involved. Conflict can enhance our empathy and understanding of ourselves and others, and lead all of us to better future choices and a more complete healing from the process.

> **Conflict can enhance our empathy and understanding of ourselves and others, and lead all of us to better future choices and a more complete healing from the process.**

∞§∞

The 5 R's Form a Circle

The first two R's, Relationship and Respect, are the keys to conflict prevention. It helps us treat everyone with respect when we deeply value relationships with others and with ourselves and recognize the worth they hold in our lives. These two keys, Relationship and Respect, lead to happiness in life.

> **By stepping up first to take responsibility for our behavior, that very act encourages others to do the same.**

The next two R's, Responsibility and Repair, are the keys to making things right when relationships experience the inevitable

144

challenges. By stepping up first to take responsibility for our behavior, that very act encourages others to do the same. And we show ourselves as honorable when we take direct action to repair any harm we have caused another, even if we did not intend the harm.

The last R, Reintegration, brings us to our higher self as it calls us to move towards forgiveness and acknowledge another's new learning, to receive back the prodigal son. In doing that not only is the other person restored to the community, but we enlarge our heart's capacity for compassion at the same time. When we have completed the reintegration process, we are back in right relationship, which brings us full circle.

"Care"ful Listening

There is a basic principle of conflict resolution that says the presenting problem is likely not to be the *real* problem. People may not know what's really bothering them when they get triggered by a seemingly inconsequential thing that suddenly bursts into a BIG deal. The process of careful listening, without responding, while the other person

> **There is a basic principle of conflict resolution that says the presenting problem is likely not to be the *real* problem.**

explores what's bothering him, or while you unpeel the layers in your own mind if you're doing this with yourself, allows time to get to the core issues. It is essential that no one is jumping in with challenges or judgments. They are just listening, intent only on understanding. This kind of listening is required to resolve issues at a core level, not just "treat the symptoms," glossing over or making nice. If a problem is resolved at the core level, it doesn't keep

145

showing up again and again, which makes it worth the time it takes to bring a case to Circle.

∞§∞

A Principal Speaks of RJ

I was at a meeting for school personnel when the conversation turned to discipline and an administrator gave this spontaneous testimony.

> *There was this group of girls in my middle school who were in my office all the time. They harassed each other; they harassed other students; they harassed their teachers. I had given them a good talking to, sent them to the counselors, assigned in-school detentions, and I had even suspended them. Then I decided to take them to LCJP and try restorative justice. That was 8 weeks ago, and I haven't had a lick of trouble with them since.*

∞§∞

Simple May Not Be Easy

The language of RJ offers us a fairly straight forward, simple process to resolve conflicts with a focus on restoring or creating right relationships. Just because it is a simple set of steps does not mean it will come naturally at first, but as all RJ practitioners know, it can become a habit, just the way we operate in the world. When I spilled the blueberry drink on that car, it only took a split second to know exactly what I needed to do; then only a few minutes more to do it and be on my way. But most of us have become accustomed to abdicating responsibility, blaming others or circumstances or fate— whatever is handy; defending ourselves and judging others. RJ won't let us get away with those bad habits. We are attached to our behaviors, and we define ourselves by our behavior patterns – *"I'm a direct person. I'll tell you what's on my mind."* *"I don't trust easily."* *"I don't get mad often, but watch out when I do."* Behavior change takes commitment, and with commitment and persistence, old habits are replaced by the impulse to act with integrity, and new habits are formed.

Again, this process is not therapy; it does not ask us to explore all our motives and behavior patterns; it just asks us to replace some dysfunctional habits with authentic ones. RJ begins quite simply by asking us to take responsibility for our behavior at all times, but especially when we are in conflict or dealing with a sensitive issue, and treat ourselves and others with respect.

> **RJ begins quite simply by asking us to take responsibility for our behavior at all times, but especially when we are in conflict or dealing with a sensitive issue, and treat ourselves and others with respect.**

And it suggests that we need to take responsibility for our own behavior *before* we expect anyone else to do the same. It asks that we put a priority on forming strong, healthy relationships, and that we listen deeply and tell our story honestly, without excuses; it asks that we repair harm when we have caused harm, and help others understand what we need from them to feel restored when we have been harmed, and that we make a place at the table for those who have taken action to make things right. It is just simply 5 R's – relationship, respect, responsibility, repair, reintegration.

Chapter 11
Reintegration — The Fifth R

There is balm in Gilead, to make the wounded whole.
There is a balm in Gilead to heal the sin sick soul.

—African American Spiritual

For the restorative process to be complete, the offender, and any others who may have felt alienated, must be accepted back into the community. Reintegration is realized when all persons have put the wrongdoing behind them and moved on into new roles in the community that recognize their worth and the importance of the new learning that has been accomplished. The person having shown himself to be an honorable person through acceptance of responsibility and repair of harm, has transformed the criminal act into a sacred wound, the kind that, when healed, becomes a valuable teacher. At the reintegration point, all parties are back in right relationship with each other and with the community. This reintegration process is the final step in achieving wholeness, of returning to the first R, Relationship.

> **The person, having shown himself to be honorable through acceptance of responsibility and repair of harm, has transformed the criminal act into a sacred wound, the kind that, when healed, becomes a valuable teacher.**

Forgiveness Is a Sacred Act

When the prodigal son returned home, he was not met with suspicion and required to regain trust. He was received with open arms and a feast was made to celebrate his return. The lessons of this parable are profound and teach us about the joy that comes for all when forgiveness is achieved. Forgiveness is the ultimate foundation for reintegration, but sometimes we can only take steps in that direction and plant seeds that may later blossom into forgiveness.

At a conference of a victim advocacy group, a keynote speaker referred to forgiveness as the "F" word. At first that sounded bizarre to me, but as I listened and learned, I came to a deeper understanding.

When someone is profoundly wounded, it is not just one thing that needs to be healed or one thing to be forgiven. A victim may come to a place of forgiveness only to awaken later to a deeper layer of pain that needs to be unpacked, and the whole cycle starts over again. This process may repeat for years, a lifetime or more. Everyone must come to forgiveness in their own way and in their own time. Forgiveness cannot be forced; in fact, it is tricky even to encourage it as it can be such a tender sore that even the gentlest pressure may smart, leaving the victim feeling re-victimized. As children we were taught to "forgive and forget," but to a victim in deep pain, that may feel like their wounds are being treated as trivial which adds another layer of abuse. Victims need permission not to forgive, not until they are fully ready, if ever.

Every so often, I see a story in the news of an African American woman, usually a grandmother, who has lost a child or grandchild to some heinous violence, and the story focuses on her forgiveness of the offender. Those stories touch our hearts and make us wonder how a person arrives at such a profound spiritual perspective, like Christ on the cross, asking forgiveness for his persecutors. There are likely experiences of compassion that precede forgiveness, explained Interfaith Minister Reverend Marilee Baccich when I told her I had not yet reached a place of forgiveness around my brother's suicide. I do feel moments of deep compassion where I seem to touch some bit of his despair, but later I feel angry again and know there are more layers yet to unfold. Every one of those moments of compassion plants another seed. If I hold hope for those seeds of forgiveness I planted to grow someday, and I water them regularly with empathy and love, they will send out roots and blossom in my heart. We have the capacity to cultivate our higher emotions or be victims of our baser ones. It may not transform quickly, but, if we allow for that possibility, in time we can shift.

> **We have the capacity to cultivate our higher emotions or be victims of our baser ones.**

∞§∞

Reintegration Completes the Circle

When I was a teacher and students would return to my classroom after a suspension or expulsion, I would greet them at the door to try to bring some balm to the sting of having to walk back in that door and across that room, feeling all eyes on them. We all knew they were being watched at every turn; we could feel someone just waiting for a misstep. And it usually came, as that very expectation conjures the reality. Now, imagine returning to school where there is a team welcoming you back, reminding you of your value by telling you how much you have been missed, believing in your success—that is the Spirit of Reintegration. Just imagine, for a moment, the difference it can make.

At the stage of testing the agreement, the facilitator asks the Circle, "If he does these things, will it satisfy you? Will you allow him back into your good graces?" Spelling this out deliberately helps the Circle to understand their obligation to receive him back, and emphasizes for the offender that completing the agreement is his road back into his community and the path to restore his self respect. Before we close the Circle, it helps the offender to hear that others are trusting him to be good to his word. Paul Zak suggests, "Acts of trust can inspire oxytocin (the hormone associated with social behavior) and trustworthiness in others."[28] Even our biochemistry, it appears, conspires to support our collective and interdependent moral evolution.

> **Even our biochemistry, it appears, conspires to support our collective and interdependent moral evolution.**

∞§∞

A Taste of Reintegration

In the RATE (Restorative Alternative to Expulsion) process, we hold a Reintegration Circle on or near the completion date of the agreement. Two young men who came to the program as offender and victim of an assault had found their way back to friendship since the first Circle. The mother of the boy who was assaulted didn't want her son wearing a "victim" label at school; she wanted the boys to be seen together at school as a message to the peer group that they had worked things out. They had spent time at each other's homes and their families had gotten comfortable with the friendship. After the Reintegration Circle, the victim's father crossed the room to the offender's father and said, "You and your family are

welcome at my home anytime." With those words, I felt
assured that reintegration was complete.

At another Reintegration Circle, a Latina tearfully lamented
the fact that she did not have an extended family, that she, her
kids, and her mom, who all lived together, were "all we have."
My heart was deeply touched by two community members who
reached out. "You are a beautiful Latina queen," one of them
said, "You can join in with my family." Another offered to
invite all of them next time his family had a barbeque.
Sometimes it is not the victim whose forgiveness restores. In
this case it took the community members to bring
reintegration, not only to the offender, but to this whole
family.

∞§∞

Growing Beyond the Past

At www.whitebison.org there are wisdom teachings
available at no cost by signing up for email, daily meditations
written by Native American elders. A recent one written by
Cochise "Like Ironweed" of the Chiricahua Apache read, "As I
make mistakes, let me see them as lessons. Guide me. When I
see others make mistakes, let me honor them for where they
are." It is a custom among some Native American tribes, when
a person receives a major life lesson, they may be given a new
name as a way of honoring the significance of the wisdom
gained, the new person they became. This ritual elevates
reintegration to its highest form.

The opposite of offering forgiveness is harboring a desire
for revenge. It is said that revenge is like taking a daily dose of
poison hoping it will kill someone else. In the practice of

153

forgiveness, we contribute significantly to our own well being as well as that of another. Forgiveness is the only way to free ourselves of the toxin; however, the act of forgiveness does not expunge the history. It doesn't just wipe the experience away as though it never happened. In the wisdom that comes from having learned this lesson well, we hold a deeper understanding that may inform us in ways that will prevent having to learn this lesson again.

There is a wonderful teaching tale from a Native American storyteller about a man and a snake.

A man was walking down the road on a very cold, wintry day. He was hurrying along, prodded by visions of the warm fire that awaited him. He saw a stick in the road and as he stepped over it, he saw it was a snake. He looked down and the snake spoke to him.

"Brother, please help me. I am so cold, frozen nearly through."

"But how can I help you, Little Brother" he asked.
"Put me inside your shirt. The warmth of your skin will bring life back to me."

"I can't do that. You might bite me, and then I would die."

"Oh, no," said Snake. "I promise I won't bite you. I promise! And if you leave me here I will surely die."

"Well, okay, but just for a short while as I walk the rest of the way to my home."

The man picked up the snake and put him next to his skin. As he walked, he could feel Snake coming back to life, making small movement. Then suddenly, he felt the piercing bite as Snake sank his fangs into the tender skin of his belly.

"Snake," he cried, "What have you done? You promised."

"Well, you knew I was a snake when you picked me up!"

When we forgive, our radar, our intuition, may operate at a keener level, uncluttered by the shadow of our pain. The lessons sometimes harden us to others, but it is possible for them to open us to others without being naïve. A psychologist once told me that past behavior is the most reliable predictor of future behavior. While it is important to open our hearts to allow space for people to make better future choices, it may be unwise to disregard the past. I may give a job to an embezzler who has done his time and repaired the harm, but I'm not going to make him the budget director.

While it is important to open our hearts to allow space for people to make better future choices, it may be unwise to disregard the past.

Shame Scars the Soul

Without reintegration, the wrongdoer may well experience shame over the event for the rest of his life, and that kind of underlying shame may be more damaging than we realize. Shame can have profoundly destructive impacts, and yet we continue to use shame to socialize children and as a response to wrongdoing. It is clearly demonstrated in our prison systems where the person's most surface level of individuality is stripped away and replaced by

155

institutional garb, not to mention the deeper levels of denigration. Something similar happens, too, when students are expelled from school; most never return to graduate. As humans have socially evolved, we have relinquished such practices of public shaming as the pillory that locked a person's head and hands in a wooden frame in the town square.

It is time to re-examine the assumed benefits of shaming as a way to elicit behavioral conformity. Not only do we inflict its curse on others, we regularly give ourselves a good dose of private shaming. Ironically, victims of sex abuse and marital infidelity are consumed with shame though they were not the instigators of the wrongdoing. Shame wounds us on a primal level. It comes from a base level of our consciousness, and its cruelty is unparalleled in the damage it can cause.

> **Shame wounds us on a primal level. It comes from a base level of our consciousness, and its cruelty is unparalleled in the damage it can cause.**

One reason we still use such strategies is that we may not know others; we keep doing the same thing, even in the face of overwhelming evidence of its ineffectiveness, such as prison recidivism rates of 70% or higher, because we do not know what else to do.

Restorative justice offers much more promising results. With the completion of the 5th R, Reintegration, offenders may reclaim their self-respect and dignity. Without the burden of shame dragging them down, they are more likely to believe in their ability to be an accepted, member of the community. Shame perpetuates wrongdoing; reintegration mitigates it.

> **Shame perpetuates wrongdoing; reintegration mitigates it.**

∞§∞

TIPS: The Language of Reintegration

• **Extend a welcome.** When people return, especially after a "required absence," it is always appropriate to welcome them back. Sometimes we may feel awkward and do not know what to say, so we do not say anything. A simple, "*Welcome back*" feels much better than silence.

• **Tell them what you've missed in their absence.** In the case where someone returns, such as suspended or expelled students, let them know what you missed about them. It makes the statement more real than a general statement that we missed you, though general statements aren't bad if they are sincere. "*I really missed your sense of humor. The class just was not as much fun without you here.*"

• **Forgiveness.** If you are ready to forgive, it is important to use the words that convey what you do and do not mean. "*I want you to know that I have forgiven you for spreading those ugly rumors about me. I understand that you were just trying to get back at me for going out with Tom. It may take some time before I feel like I can trust you again with my private thoughts. I think you have learned from this experience and you aren't likely to do that kind of thing again. At least I hope you won't do vengeful things to me or to anyone ever again.*"

Chapter 12
There Is a Place for You in the Circle

Shifting the balance or tipping the scales from vulnerability to resilience may happen as a result of one person or one opportunity.

—Bonnie Benard

If you are still reading to the last chapter of this book, you are likely to be at least interested if not inspired by the concepts of restorative justice. It is not uncommon for people to recognize the restorative way at a deep level and be drawn to its inherent rightness. When this happens, they want to embrace it more fully. If you are interested in moving more deeply into the restorative way, you will want to read on. This last chapter is offered to assist you in bringing the restorative concepts to use in your life and to suggest ways that you can support the fuller integration of restorative practices into our society.

∞§∞

Walking the Talk

One of the best ways to bring restorative justice to your life is to live by the guidance of the 5 R's. The 5 R's are the ideals I want to manifest in my life, and some days I come closer than others. Some of the R's are not well integrated into our society. For example, our culture doesn't measure up well on the third R—Responsibility. From elected officials and corporate officers to our court systems, there is no shortage of models for shifting responsibility rather than owning it. I had to work hard

> **One of the best ways to bring restorative justice to your life is to live by the guidance of the 5 R's.**

to break the habit of blaming "time" for my priority choices. "I didn't have time" is something I now try to avoid saying. Many of us have work to do in the area of taking personal responsibility and teaching it to our children.

It can be revealing to take a look at your life from the perspective of the 5 R's. You might give yourself a 1 - 5 rating on each of the R's to identify areas of strength and challenge.

1. **Relationships** – Do I place strong value on sustaining relationships? What examples could others find in my life that show friends and family matter deeply to me? When I get my feelings hurt by someone, do I retract from the relationship or do I muster the courage to speak to him about it? Do I have to be angry to have this conversation at all, which risks starting it with blaming? Can I open the conversation in a warm and accepting way that honors what I value in the other person? Do I let the people know what I value about them, what I see as their assets? Can I approach my hurt feelings in way that strengthens the relationship? Do I take steps to identify and speak the harm I am feeling from him using "I" statements? Do I ask for the apology or other repair that I need? Do I inquire about what he needs?

2. **Respect** – How do I show respect to my friends and family? What does respect mean to me? Have I asked my spouse, my kids or grandkids, my friends what respect means to them? Can I point to things I do on a regular basis that are respectful of

160

others? How do I show respect for myself? Is there a secret monster hiding in my closet that I have been unwilling to address? What steps could I take that would increase my self-respect?

3. **Responsibility** – How well do I model taking personal responsibility? Do I tend to blame things on others, on a lack of resources, on the other driver, on the dog? Am I willing to take responsibility for harm and try to repair it when I did not intend the harm? Are there areas in my life, such as being consistently late or failing to recycle, where I tend to shift responsibility by making excuses? Could I shift that pattern by accepting and owning my "imperfections"? How would that impact others? It feels like a huge load has been lifted when we simply own our mistakes or our part in a problem and then take steps toward repair.

4. **Repair** – What are some words I could use to ask a spouse or a friend what I could do to make things right? Once I find those words, I hold the keys that generally help to resolve relationship problems. What if the "harmed" person wants the proverbial pound of flesh in return? I will first listen fully without any attempts to justify my behavior. After persons feel fully heard, they tend to be more willing to negotiate a fair and just agreement to repair harm. If needed, would I contact a mediator for assistance? Can I explain this repair concept to a child? As obvious as this may sound to adults, at LCJP we encounter lots of young ones who do not understand they can do things to repair harm. We can teach children and youth that relationships may be mended, that we can learn from our mistakes and be better, wiser for them. I love the quote from George Washington: "Good judgment comes from experience, and experience comes from bad judgment."

5. **Reintegration** – R's 1 and 2 are about conflict prevention. R's 3 and 4 are about justice, and number 5 is all about mercy. Our capacity for compassion and mercy are what advance our soul's progress and make our world better. This can be a really tough concept, and, for some of us, it can take a lifetime to learn. For others, it seems to be almost second nature. How do I rate myself in this arena? Once someone has been willing to complete the restorative steps of responsibility and repair, am I able to offer them a handshake or a hug?

> R's 1 and 2 are about conflict prevention. R's 3 and 4 are about justice, and number 5 is all about mercy.

Now that you have assessed your standing with the 5 R's, it is time to celebrate your areas of strength and consider if you are ready to set some related goals or take specific steps to address your challenges. The story that follows encourages me to look deeper into my own heart.

∞§∞

Repairing Our Self Respect

"Disciplining yourself to do what you know is right and important, although difficult, is the highroad to pride, self-esteem, and personal satisfaction."
—Brian Tracy

Self-respect may be the most important of all qualities to cultivate. As restorative justice practitioners and advocates, we guide others to be respectful and take personal responsibility. As

> Self-respect may be the most important of all qualities to cultivate.

162

we hold others accountable in these ways, it calls us to rise to the same standard. This young man's courageous personal journey superbly demonstrates self-respect and personal responsibility at a level that inspires me.

Joshua's Story

Joshua is a young man who is now in his 30's. I have known him from birth though we never lived nearby so years would go by between our visits. As far back as I can recall, Joshua was challenged by stuttering. Joshua says he realized in childhood that he stuttered, and even attended speech therapy though he has little memory of the actual sessions. What he does recall were some painful episodes in school and college that left him feeling embarrassment and shame. In his mid 20's he recognized that he wasn't dating as much as he'd like and associated that with his stuttering. With the help of his mother administering transcendental kinesiology, he gave voice to his inner turmoil and formulated it into a question, "Why do I stutter?"

In pursuit of that question, he got a fellowship to work at the National Institutes of Health with the preeminent geneticist who was pursuing the gene for stuttering. Shortly thereafter he entered graduate school at the University of Maryland where he continued to delve into the science of stuttering. When that would take him no farther, he came to recognize there was a grander answer to his question, namely his stuttering provided the understanding and passion to move him into a fulfilling career in stuttering education and treatment. Today he's pursuing a masters degree in speech pathology, working in a children's speech clinic, and driving a car with the license plate "SSTUTRR." And I hear he now is engaged to a lovely young woman.

Joshua moved into his "problem" and became so thoroughly clear about it that his pain was transmuted to passion. It is a pleasure to spend time in conversation with him. Instead of sitting uncomfortably as he takes the time he needs for fluency, I am deeply impressed by his wealth of knowledge, and his willingness to share his many insights. His comfort with himself makes me completely comfortable with him, and his multi-layered wisdom about stuttering gives permission for any question to be asked. He is a fabulously aware, caring young man, and our world is a far better place — especially for people who stutter — because he's in it. Not everyone can or should turn a challenge into a life work, but the big lesson from Joshua is to move into, not away from, what bothers us. When we find the courage to face the very demons that plague us, we can make peace within. In his own words, "It is from here that we are able to empower ourselves, and nothing is more freeing than making peace within and finding our strength."

...the big lesson from Joshua is to move into, not away from, what bothers us.

If you plan to be a restorative justice practitioner, it is imperative that you walk the talk. Sometimes when I am faced with some aspect of myself that feels scary to me, I think of Joshua and recalling his brave heart transforms my fear to a smile.

Conducting Informal Restorative Circles
~ Try This At Home ~

The 5 R's can guide us in how we think about things and how we communicate with others. To help you speak in a restorative way, each of the chapters on the 5 R's ends with suggestions of language that promotes a restorative approach. These are merely suggestions to get you started. It is most important that you find your own words, ones that feel comfortable coming out of your mouth. Once you hold the 5 R's clearly in your mind, it becomes surprisingly easy to find these

> **The 5 R's, the 3 questions, and the 3 perspectives are the essential components of your restorative toolbox.**

words. In addition to the 5 R's, there are the 3 questions: what harm was done; what repair is needed; who is responsible for the repair? And lastly, there are 3 primary points of view to be considered: the victim (and family), the offender (and family), and the community. The 5 R's, the 3 questions, and the 3 perspectives are the essential components of your restorative toolbox.

When we bring these basic concepts together and put them into words, we are practicing restorative justice. When there are legal consequences involved, I do not recommend that you facilitate a justice Circle with the level of exposure you have gotten from this book. However, you may use these ideas to conduct informal Circles, such as within your family to resolve sibling challenges. Start with simpler concerns or problems and get experience before tackling difficult or longstanding issues. **It is unwise to do a Circle if you have concerns about the safety of the participants.**

- Sit in an open circle or around the kitchen table so that everyone is in plain view of each other.
- Establish some ground rules. Everyone must be treated with respect. Make agreements about privacy, truth telling, and only one person speaking at a time.
- Say that each person will get a chance to speak without interruption. If any of the ground rules are violated, it is your responsibility as the facilitator to see that they are followed. You can use a talking piece to help curb interruptions if that is a challenge.
- State the concern or problem in the simplest possible way, being cautious not to blame or shame anyone. Establish that your purpose is to solve the problem in a way that repairs any harm to relationships.
- Each person tells about the harm he perceives and what he thinks would make things right.
- Ask each person who is being expected to repair harm what she thinks she should do. This could be everyone in the Circle.
- Negotiate who will do what by when until you come to agreement. Decide when you need to check back in to see how things are going. Write down agreements and have everyone sign that they agree.

If your first attempt at a family Circle doesn't go as hoped, do not give up. Simply end the Circle in as neutral a way as possible. For example, *"It looks to me like we aren't quite ready to follow the ground rules today. For now, we'll just have to do things* **If you find yourself in a situation where you do not know what to do, just do the most loving thing you can think of at that moment.**

my way. Maybe, if you want to, we can try again at another time to work things out in a way that everyone has a say in what happens."

I was at an international restorative justice conference listening to a man who trained parolees to go into violent, gang-ridden projects in a large, urban area. He provided them a job, suited them up in red blazers and gave them the task of forming relationships with young wanna-be gangsters for the ultimate purpose of helping them see and opt for better choices. It was an impressive program on many levels, but the thing I remember most is his final advice to them. After completing their training when they were about to hit the streets, he told them, *"We've talked a lot about the things you're likely to encounter out there, and certainly things will come up that we haven't covered. If you find yourself in a situation where you do not know what to do, just do the most loving thing you can think of at that moment."* I think that may be the finest piece of advice I have ever heard. If you do not know what to do in your Circle, you might ask yourself, "What is the most loving thing I can do in this moment?"

You can also consult Appendix 2 for further insight into using a restorative approach to conflict resolution. Try not to be too discouraged by one failed attempt. Circle process is unfamiliar to most people from industrialized countries, but with an incentive, like the potential to avoid being grounded, and a little experience to normalize the process, it can be a wonderful tool for parents, grandparents, teachers and others who believe in the power of a restorative approach.

Facilitating Formal Justice Circles

When I facilitate formal justice Circles, I generally have a guide, or script, in my lap to keep me on track. Some restorative justice facilitators find the use of a guide distracting, disconnecting them from the participants. I find just the opposite is true for me. I like to have my full attention on the people in the Circle and not on remembering what comes next, or specific details of the process. The script can also help Circle participants feel more secure that this is not just a free flowing process; there is a plan and someone is in charge of following it. I am not providing a Circle script with this book, because it has long been our policy at LCJP not to give out scripts without training.

There is an art and a science to facilitating restorative justice Circles. The science is quite simple; it is contained in the script that is derived from the principles, values and practices discussed throughout this book. The art, however, is far more complex, as that involves managing the human dynamics of the Circle. It would be irresponsible, even unethical, to give you tools that would create a false sense of safety, that could actually do harm, without also having the training to use them properly. If you are interested in becoming a restorative justice facilitator, connect with the closest RJ program in your area. Find out if you can become a volunteer and how you may get training. If you cannot find a program nearby, you are in exactly the position I was when I first learned of restorative justice. You may just have to initiate one. There is guidance to do that, in an earlier book I coauthored called *Restorative Justice in Action: A Program Implementation Manual from the Longmont Community Justice Partnership.* That book is available at www.LCJP.org/products. There may be other support as well in your vicinity. I find the restorative justice practitioners' community to be helpful and open to providing as much assistance to start up programs as their resources permit.

The *Context of Care* Diagram

In 2009 Kappy Hall and I formed a business called *ReSolutionaries, Inc.* (www.resolutionariesinc.com) to assist schools in implementing restorative practices, specializing in student-led restorative processes. As we began presenting restorative approaches to school staffs and students, we wanted a visual reminder depicting the 5 R's working together with the 3 Questions. We created the Context of Care diagram (Diagram 2) to illustrate the interrelationship of the components of the restorative approach. A context of care emerges when we use the principles of the 5 R's and the restorative questions to focus on harm and repair rather than punishment and shaming.

Imbedded in the center of the diagram are the 3 questions articulated by Howard Zehr, the "grandfather" of restorative justice in America. After training in the essential components of the restorative way, a poster of this diagram can serve as a visual reminder of what we need to be mindful of in doing any restorative practice.

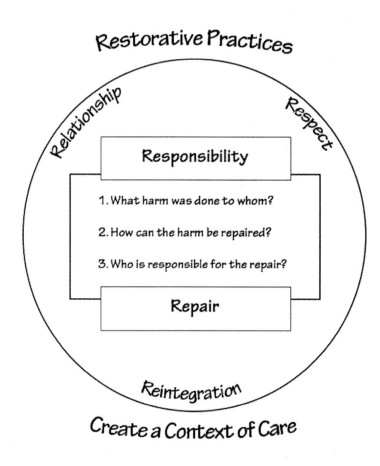

Diagram 2. The Context of Care

Another Lesson from My Students: A Context of Care Opens the Heart's Door

Remember those students I spoke about at the beginning of this book in the Introduction and other chapters? The alternative high school students whose lives were so powerfully impacted by violence; violence was done to them and they, in turn, did harm to others. They are the ones who taught me about the power of providing a context of care for our interactions with others. The restorative justice process, based on the 5 R's, does this exquisitely.

My class was what is referred to as a "school within a school." It was more like a class within a large high school, and I was the sole teacher for 15 students. We were housed in a church basement a block away from the main school, which provided us a great deal of autonomy. When problems arose, we sat in a circle and figured out the best solution together. I wish I had had the 5 R's in those days, as I was figuring it out as I went. My students went to the high school campus for lunch and physical education. Many of the adults at the high school feared my students, and some were annoyed that resources were allocated to provide for them. My students, in turn, resented those teachers and rarely missed an opportunity to aggravate them. I was regularly called to the office to deal with incidents sparked by this dynamic. I asked the students why their behavior could be so lovely in our class and so obnoxious at those times. The answer was always some version of, "Teach, if the rest of the world would just treat us like you do, there wouldn't be a problem."

At first this baffled me, because I knew I was not easy on these kids. I was firm about accountability, and I never let them get away with malicious or even unkind behavior. But they were talking about the context of care that existed in our classroom. It was not about how tough or easy someone was toward them, it was really about their perception of whether or not the other person cared about them. In our class, everyone was treated with respect, and caring about each other was non-negotiable. They would accept tough accountability as long as it existed within this context of care. Care opens our heart's door. It is what allows us entry into another's world. Feeling truly cared about by another is a crucial step in developing a trusting relationship. This diagram is a reminder of the essential ingredients for creating and sustaining a context of care.

∞§∞

The Power of a Circle

The graphic depicts the restorative justice concepts that create a context of care embedded in a circle. It is no accident that restorative processes are conducted in circle arrangements. In a circle there is no hierarchy. There is no beginning or end. There is no hiding, as everyone is fully visible to each other. The circle is the perfect shape to facilitate an open, respectful and truthful communication.

I recently spent a few days at a friend's home to offer support as she recovered from an illness. The "family room" was arranged with most of the comfortable furniture in a line facing a television. Not only did that make the television the focal point of the room, it also made communication difficult as we could not easily see each other's faces. I am usually a conversational person, but in that room, I was only making short grunts and groans in reaction to the television commentator's remarks as my recovering friend rested down the row in her recliner. I soon found myself bringing in a straight chair from the dining area and positioning it to obliquely face my friend. When others visited, I pulled in a few more of those dining chairs and created a little circle with my friend's lounge chair included. We created a cozy little circle and had nice visits.

In my work I have many occasions to have people sit in a Circle. Sometimes there are large numbers of people in an oblong room and the best shape we can form is more oval than round.

172

When that happens there can be a different feel to the Circle. People have to crane to see some speakers, and there are generally some people who do not make the extra effort and much of the speaker's message is lost to them. We know that more communication happens in the nonverbal messages than the verbal ones, especially the nuances of meaning. Often it is those subtle messages that contain the deeper levels of that person's truth. If you cannot fully see them, much is lost.

The dynamic is also impacted when a table is present. I have never seen research on this aspect of Circle process, and I would be interested in it. At LCJP we teach our facilitators to tell participants during the preconference meeting that there will be an open Circle with no table. For most people, the closest image they can draw upon to understand restorative justice comes from mediation, and they associate mediation with "coming to the table." The open Circle can be intimidating at first, as people may feel vulnerable. More than a few times, I

> **Deep listening needs engagement of our eyes and hearts as well as our ears and brains. In deep listening, we find the path to restoration.**

have seen a Circle participant slide his chair back until he is actually out of the Circle. I ask that the Circle stay round to support deep listening. Deep listening needs engagement of our eyes and hearts as well as our ears and brains. In deep listening, we find the path to restoration.

I believe in the power of a Circle. Any time people come together for the purpose of communication, sitting in a round circle works well. The furniture arrangement can influence the tone and the tenor of the communication. This is especially true when circle members do not know each other, or only have professional relationships. However, when doing informal Circles in homes, sitting around the kitchen table can work just fine and is often where

173

everyone is most comfortable. Be aware of the need for everyone to be fully visible to each other to facilitate comprehension of each other's full meaning. From that understanding, a collective wisdom can emerge to uncover possible solutions that would likely not have been presented or accepted without the entirety of the dialogue.

∞§∞

Restorative Justice Is a Way of Life

You have likely already concluded that restorative practices are more than Circles and about more than justice. I just saw an article by Laura Mirsky, a major documenter of the restorative justice movement, entitled "The Sanctuary Model: A Restorative Approach for Human Services Organizations." Mirsky writes," The Sanctuary Model is a non-hierarchical, highly participatory, "trauma-informed and evidence-supported" operating system for human services organizations, which helps them function in a humane, democratic and socially responsible manner and thereby provide effective treatment for clients in a clinical setting." She goes on to say, "The model is entirely congruent with restorative practices, in that it is about working with people instead of doing things to them or for them." [29]

The restorative justice movement is having a significant influence in many areas of human service work. The introduction of social action based on a set of social justice-oriented values and principles is appealing and widely applicable. I received an email yesterday from a colleague, a former environmental campaigner for Greenpeace, who is offering a workshop called "Restorative Activism." He and a partner also offer restorative divorce and restorative parenting. You can find out more about their work at www.openpathtrainings.com.

There are a number of organizations that promote social engagement whose basic beliefs and action are clearly aligned with restorative values and principles though they have never been directly associated with the restorative movement. One of these is mentoring. Research shows that mentoring practices have an excellent track record in advancing young lives based on the power of the first R, Relationship.

There are many ways you can contribute to the restorative justice movement by volunteering. If there is not a restorative justice program in your area and you are not quite up for the challenge of initiating one, consider what other organizations might be a good fit. Here is a story of how Teaching Peace became an informal mentor of sorts.

Many Trails on the "Restorative" Path

This year, for the first time, Teaching Peace had a magnificent win-win opportunity. Our local community foundation was offering internships at nonprofit agencies for young adults, and Teaching Peace received an intern. Our interviewer met applicants, and she instantly identified Flor as the right fit for our organization.

Flor is a Latina, of immigrant parents, who is as beautiful as she is talented and smart. She had just graduated from high school and was already accepted to a nearby college for the fall term. We had her for the summer — lucky us! We originally had some concerns about the possible drain on our limited resources if an intern were to require a lot of supervision. That concern evaporated as we quickly saw what a great gift she was to our organization, but it took a little longer to recognize how valuable our mentorship would be to her.

The longer Flor worked with us, the more her talents emerged. She is a gifted artist, which we first discovered when she made posters for our annual volunteer recognition party and gifts for the volunteers. I was in charge of the party that year, and, due to the economic challenges of the times, I had a $300 budget and was told to try to under spend it. I could not imagine how to accomplish that, but she did.

Flor charmed local restaurant owners into donating the food and decorations; she and some other staff made the gifts; our board president donated her beautiful home for the venue; other staff did salsa dancing demonstrations and lessons, and my friend tended our donated bar. Flor recruited her boyfriend and her sister to assist with party set up, hosting and clean up. The party was great fun, and the highlight for me was when Flor agreed to do a slam poetry performance of her original work.

The summer ended and so did her internship. Flor went on to college life, though her influence on us remains. Fortunately, we also had a chance to encourage and support her to have a successful entré to college. When she needed advice about classes to take, how to approach the "difficult" professor, balancing social life and academics, **There are ample entry points, and I urge you to jump in somewhere.** Flor had a whole group of college-educated big sisters right there for her. And the positive ripple of this relationship is beyond imagining. Whether we are helping a little one learn to read and do math, or urging an older one to college success, mentoring builds relationships, and it is one of the most "restorative" things we can ever do. There are ample entry points, and I urge you to jump in somewhere. And it can be very fun!

Flor's Poem:

It's all so crazy,
The way they're tearing their homes,
Shooting them down.
Blowing things just so big out of proportion.
Blaming things,

And pointing fingers,
At the ones whose lives,
No... they don't matter.
Whose words just don't count.
Been put down with actions so big,
It scares me just to think of that amount.
Sat there and contemplated.
Yes I have debated.
Man, let's not make things
so goddamn complicated.

My life isn't about
bimbos with their boobies inflated.
Not about big hoes
who don't know what's fornicated.
Not about sweeping or cleaning,
or kissing ass.
Nope, not about LIGHTS FLASHING.
And I mean it,
I say this with a passion.
So why should,
Mine
Theirs
Yours
Or ours
be based on something so insignificant?
Why?
Because you're African,
He's white,
She's green,
And I'm Mexican?
Because he married his man,
And she's too afraid to admit

that she's lesbian?
No...

We've all heard it before.
LET FREEDOM RING!
Listen to me scream.
This life that we live in
isn't much more than a dream.
LET FREEDOM RING!
It's crazy,
It's beautiful, and I'll say it again.
Repeat it over and over
till you get it in your head.
We've got soldiers over seas,
dropping the bombs
until they are dead.
LET FREEDOM RING!
Let's stop with the pain,
And I say it in vain.
People's bathtubs filled with meth...
Man that shit's insane.
Poisoning our children's minds
with fear and with fame.
With everything from money to games,
And people calling you names.
It's our future that we torture,
But please sweet baby,
Don't cry.
Those tears that you shed,
They're like diamonds in your eyes.
I'll keep those precious crystals,
And save them through the years.
And maybe one day,
It'll give me one reason,

That I should stay alive.
Some thrive,
while others struggling,
Day by day
Just to survive.
But until the day
All of this comes to an end.
All we can do
Is reminisce and pretend.
Love our lives forever,
Until our body goes on to descend.
LET FREEDOM RING! [30]

The Power of Personal Action

This modern time cries out for a return to the ancient wisdom of restorative justice. I have repeatedly witnessed its transformative power in Circles and understand its capacity to bring deep healing and real justice to our world. I believe that the biggest barriers to its broader implementation are public awareness and the political will to fund it. I hope we will learn from Flor to let our voices be heard. Even if our words are imperfect, our message can ring. Pass this book, and others on RJ, along to friends, educators, and elected officials. Talk about restorative justice. Explain its meaning to those who haven't heard about it yet. Acquaint yourself with examples you can point to, like the Lookout Mountain Detention Center in Golden, Colorado, where restorative justice is mending the lives of

You can be an advocate for this sane, practical, empathy-enhancing, cost-effective and results-oriented movement that brings both justice and mercy to our world.

some seriously criminal youth. And LCJP, where we are diverting hundreds of youth from "the system." Write opinion pieces for your local paper. Contact elected officials. You can be an advocate for this sane, practical, empathy-enhancing, cost-effective and results-oriented movement that brings both justice and mercy to our world.

∞§∞

Inspired Social Action

To leave a legacy of peace and social justice for our children and our children's children, we will need to join with others in inspired social action. We increase our power exponentially when we cooperate in large-scale efforts. Many hands make light work, and a playful spirit can turn any task to fun. I remember times in childhood when dreaded chores were transformed into play by the joyful spirit of girlfriends who danced and sang and joked the work into an afternoon of spirited, creative fun. There can be great joy in purposeful, collaborative action.

> **To leave a legacy of peace and social justice for our children and our children's children, we will need to join with others in inspired social action. We increase our power exponentially when we cooperate in large-scale efforts.**

Have you seen a flash mob? Wikipedia definition: "A flash mob (or flashmob) is a large group of people who assemble suddenly in a public place, perform an unusual action for a brief time, then quickly disperse. The term flash mob is generally applied only to gatherings organized via telecommunications, social media, or viral emails." Oprah's Kickoff Party for the 2009 Fall television season featured a flash mob dance that took over Chicago's Magnificent Mile as Oprah's fans performed one of the biggest dances in the world. It demonstrated to me that we have new possibilities for group action that are unlike anything that has happened before. Even ten years ago, few of us could have envisioned the fall of dictators in Africa and the Middle East that has resulted from political organizing of the populace via social networks. Social networks offer important opportunities to explore ideas and expand our understanding by synthesizing knowledge like never before possible. What an exciting time to be awake! A quick Internet search can put you in touch with numerous RJ Internet sites and blogs.

Though I sometimes call it the "Too Much Information Age," a great gift of living in this time is that the world is available to us as it has never been before. In my parents' era and previously, only a privileged few traveled far enough beyond their own culture to benefit from vastly different perspectives. Today the teachings of the world's wisdom traditions are accessible to

We live in a time where we have the means for social action commensurate to the complexity of the problems we face.

anyone who wishes to move beyond a television version of reality. And our capacity for organized, collaborative action is beyond anything an earlier community organizer could have imagined. We live in a time where we have the means for social action commensurate to the complexity of the problems we face. Not only do we have the means, but we also have the wisdom of the ages at our fingertips. We may be the ones to usher in a new era of justice, an era of justice with mercy.

I would love to hear about any inspired action you take. Please email me at Beverly@resolutionariesinc.com.

Study guides for *Teaching Peace* are available at
www.resolutionariesinc.net.

Appendix 1
Comparison of School Discipline Models

Retributive Discipline	Restorative Discipline
Offense is thought to be a violation of the law or a school rule.	Offense is thought to be harmful to another person and the community.
The school or teacher sets controls.	The involved parties set controls.
Offense is considered an individual act.	Offense is regarded as harm done to many.
Resolution is based upon top down authority determining consequences.	Resolution is decided through dialogue and negotiation with involved parties.
Goal is to punish wrongdoer.	Goal is to restore all parties to harmony.
Victims are not involved in the process.	Victims are central to the repair plan.
Community is not represented.	Community representatives participate in the process.

Offender is punished and often does not take responsibility for harmful actions.	Offender accepts responsibility for harm done and takes action to repair the harm.
Focused on offender's past behaviors.	Focused on harmful effects of offense with intent to guide future choices.
The offender's weak points are identified.	The offender's strengths are identified and used to repair the harm.
Depends on professionals for outcome.	Depends upon participation by all parties involved – a partnership.
Punishment is used to: - stop more offenses in future - change offender's behavior.	Punishment is considered: - break down of human dignity and disruptive to community relations - to make no real difference in changing future behaviors.

Appendix 2
A Restorative Justice Approach To Conflict Resolution

1. *RESPECT*
All persons are valued and treated with respect.
Respect is the foundation for creating a safe space in which **Truth** can be spoken. Ask if there are other ground rules in addition to Respect needed to ensure safety.

2. *RESPONSIBILITY*
Each person tells their version of what happened in this conflict.
Everyone needs to identify the part of the problem for which he/she can accept responsibility. Stories are told *without* interruption.

3. *RELATIONSHIPS*
Identify who was hurt and how they have been harmed.
Consider harm to people, relationships & property.

4. *REPAIR*
Identify what will repair the harm.
Each party identifies what he/she needs to repair the harm, considering harm to victim, community and offender. Agreements are made by consensus, written up and signed by all participants. Agreements specify who will do what by when.

5. *REINTEGRATION*
The final step is receiving those who have caused harm back into the community.
Once the agreement is completed, the past is surrendered and let go, making reintegration back into community possible.

Appendix 3
Apology Guidelines

In our society, when someone has harmed another, it is important that apology be made. We are proud of you for being willing to take responsibility for your behavior and apologize to those who were harmed by your action. These guidelines are intended to support you in writing a meaningful apology.

Why Apologize?

An apology may be the first step to repairing a damaged relationship. It says that you recognize that what you did was wrong, whether it was intentional or unintentional, and that you have regrets about how the other person was affected. By making apology you show that you are an honorable person and that may help the other person begin to trust you.

Why not apologize?

If an apology does not feel sincere, it can further damage the relationship. Sincerity is expressed by what you say, how you say it, and what body language you use.

The following are guidelines for making an effective apology:

- **Describe what happened in detail.** This shows the person you are apologizing to that you understand the circumstances for which you are apologizing.

    [I need to apologize to you for _____.]

- **Acknowledge the harm that was caused to the person you are apologizing to.** The person who was harmed needs to know that you recognize that their pain or embarrassment is real, even if others might have felt differently.

[I understand that this caused you to _____.]

- **Recognize the wrongdoing and take responsibility.** You need to acknowledge that, whether or not the offense was intentional, you are accountable for causing the harm.

[_____ is what I did that was wrong.]

- **State your regret.** While "I'm sorry" is generally not enough for a complete apology, it is an important part of the process.

[I am sorry that I _____ and that you were _____.]

- **State a goal to *not* act in the same manner in the future.** You should offer a clear plan or promise for improved behavior and what you intend to do the future in similar situations.

[In the future, I will _____.

Appendix 4
Asset Survey

The questions in his survey are designed to illicit strengths, or assets, of young people. The numbers in parentheses at the end of each question are coded to William Glassers' 4 Needs of a Healthy Personality: 1 = love and belonging, 2 = worth and recognition, 3 = fun, 4 = Empowerment, which is highly associated with having and exercising choices. This coding can help you identify areas of strength and challenge.

1. Name one or two adults who care about you and help you to succeed. (1)

2. How do they help support your success? (1)

3. Do you believe you have friends you can count on to be there for you? How many? (1)

4. Who do you care about? (1)

5. What are you good at (what do you do well)? (2,3)

6. What types of jobs do you like to do, or what service to the community interests you? (3,4)

7. What do you like to learn about in school? (3,4)

8. What do you like to learn about that is not taught in school? (3)

9. What makes you special or different from other people? (2)

10. What do you do to help yourself when you're feeling alone, nervous, or upset? (4)

11. What do you do in your life to stay healthy? (4)

12. What organizations do you belong to (scouts, church, clubs at school)? (1)

13. Who do you help and how do you help them? (1,2)

14. When do you feel valued and needed? (1,2)

15. When have you ever had a chance to be a leader? How did you like it? (2/3)

16. What are your goals? Where would you like to be in two, five, ten years? (4)

17. If you had three wishes, what would they be? (4)

18. If you had the power to change the world, what would you do? (4)

19. Is there anything else that you would like people to know about you? (4)

Notes

Preface

1. Ross, Rupert. *Dancing with a Ghost; exploring Indian reality.* (Toronto, Canada: Reed Books, 1992), p. 163. This is my favorite book on Native justice. I often quote from it.

Chapter 1 – The Ancients

2. Underwood, Paula. *The Walking People: a native American oral history.* (San Anselmo, CA: A Tribe of Two Press and the Center for Noetic Sciences, 1993), pp 53-4. This book recounts the native oral history of the crossing of the Bering Straits after a tsunami swept away the tribal leaders. The people created a new system of governance that rested with the collective intelligence of the clan rather than investing authority with a single individual. It is powerful and poetic in its content and in its adherence to Native language stylistic forms. It is a stunning achievement. The capitalization and forms quoted from this book are taken directly as they appear in *The Walking People.*

Chapter 2 – The Moderns

3. Benson, Peter, Judy Galbraith M.A., and Pamela Espeland. *What Kids Need to Succeed: proven, practical ways to raise good kids.* (Minneapolis, MN: Free Spirit publishing, 1998.)

Chapter 3 – Relationship – The First R

4. Goleman, Daniel. *Emotional Intelligence.* (New York, NY: Bantam Books, 1995.)

5. Head, Marian. *The Revolutionary Agreements.* (Niwot, CO: Marlin Press, 2005), p. 59.

6. Fisher, Roger and William Ury. *Getting to Yes.* (New York, NY: Penguin Group, 1991.)

7. Ruiz, Don Miguel. *The Four Agreements.* (San Rafael, CA: Amber-Allen Publishing, Inc, 1997), p. 47.

Chapter 4 – A Ripple in the Pond

8. Perkins, John and Shakaim Mariano Shakai Ijisam Chumpi. *Spirit of the Shuar: wisdom of the last unconquered people of the Amazon.* (Rochester, VT: Destiny Books, 2001), pp. 44-58.

Chapter 5 – Respect – The Third R

9. Ross, Rupert. *Dancing with a Ghost: exploring Indian reality.* (Toronto, Ontario: McClelland and Stewart, Inc., 1992), p viii.

10. Nathanson, Donald L. *Shame and Pride: affect, sex, and the birth of the self.* (New York, NY: W.W. Norton and Company, 1992), pp 136.

11. Gilligan , James. *Violence; reflections of a national epidemic.* (New York, NY: Vintage Books, Random House, 1997), pp 419-20.

12. Olmert, Meg Daley. *Made for Each Other: the biology of the human- animal bond.* (Philadelphia, PA: A Merloyd Lawrence Book, 2009), pp 108-9.

13. Rosenberg, Marshall B. *Nonviolent Communication: a language of life.* (Encinitas, CA: Puddledancer Press, 2003), pp 113-128.

Chapter 6 – The Restorative Way

14. Zehr, Howard. *A New Focus for Crime and Justice: changing lenses.* (Scottsdale, PA: Harold Press, 1990), p. 181

15. Magid, Ken and Carole McKelvey. *High Risk: children without a conscience.* (New York, NY: Bantam Books, 1989), pp 6-7.
16. Olmert, *ibid*, p 110.
17. Palmer, Parker. *To Know As We Are Known: Education as a spiritual journey.* (San Francisco, CA: Harper San Francisco, 1993), p. xxiiv.

Chapter 7 – Responsibility – The Third R
18. Olmert, *ibid*, pp 108-9.

Chapter 8 – Why the Restorative Justice Movement is Spreading
19. Hanh, Thich Nhat. *Peace is Every Step: the path of mindfulness in everyday life.* (New York, NY: Bantam Books, 1991). p. 87.
20. Karp, David R. and Thom Allena. *Restorative Justice on the College Campus: promoting student growth and responsibility, and reawakening the spirit of campus community.* Springfield, IL: Charles C. Thomas Publishers, LTD, 2004.)
21. Braithwaite, John. *Session at the International Institute of Restorative Practices Conference in Veldhoven*, the Netherlands, 2003.
22. Underwood, Paula, *ibid.*
23. Hubbard, Barbara Marx. www.evolve.org

Chapter 9 - Repair – The Fourth R
24. Olmert, *ibid*, p. 6.
25. Ross, *Ibid*, pp 3-4.

Chapter 10 - The Language of Restorative Justice

26. Olmert, *ibid*, p. 107.
27. Olmert, *ibid*, p. 6.

Chapter 11 - Reintegration – The Fifth R

28. Olmert, *ibid*, p. 60.

Chapter 12 – There Is a Place in the Circle for You

29. Mirsky, Laura. "The Sanctuary Model: a restorative approach for human services organizations." See: IIRP.org/library.
30. Marquez, Flor. "Let Freedom Ring." Unpublished poem.

Suggested Readings by Topic

Peace Making and Conflict Resolution

Carter, Jimmy. *Talking Peace: a vision for the next generation.* New York, NY: Dutton Children's Books, 1993.

Fisher, Roger and William Ury. *Getting to Yes.* New York, NY: Penguin Books, 1984.

Houston, Jean with Margaret Rubin. *Manual for the PeaceMaker: an Iroquois legend to heal self and society.* Wheaton, IL: Theosophical Publishing House, 1995.

Lederach, John Paul. *The Little Book of Conflict Transformation.* Intercourse, PA: Good Books, 2003,

_____. *Building Peace: sustainable reconciliation in divided societies.* Washington, DC: United States Institute of Peace Press, 1997.

_____. *Preparing for Peace: conflict transformation across cultures.* Syracuse, NY: Syracuse University Press, 1995.

Lynch, Dudley and Paul L. Kordis. *Strategy of the Dolphin: Scoring a Win in a Chaotic World.* New York, NY: Fawcett Columbine, 1988.

Parry, Danaan. *Warriors of the Heart: a handbook for conflict resolution.* Cooperstown, NY: Sunstone Publications, 1991.

Russell, Bertrand. *Power: a new social analysis.* London: Unwin Books, 1938.

195

Ury, William. *The Third Side*. New York, NY: Penguin Books, 2000.

Wilmot, William and Joyce Hocker. *Interpersonal Conflict*. New York, NY: McGraw-Hill, 2001.

Restorative Justice and Talking Circles

Baldwin, Christina. *Calling the Circle: the first and future culture*. New York,NY: Bantam Books, 1994.

Braithwaite, John. *Crime, Shame and Reintegration*. Cambridge, UK: Cambridge University Press, 1999.

_____. *Restorative Justice and Responsive Regulation*. Oxford, UK: Oxford University Press, 2002.

Breton, Denise and Stephen Lehman. *The Mystic Heart of Justice: restoring wholeness in a broken world*. West Chester, PA: Chrysalis Books, 2001.

Bazemore, Gordon and Mara Schiff. *Restorative Community Justice; repairing harm and transforming communities*. Cincinnati, OH: Anderson Publishing Co., 2001.

Pranis, Kay. *The Little Book of Circle Processes: a new/old approach to peacemaking*. Intercourse, PA: Good Books, 2005.

Pranis, Kay, Barry Stuart, and Mark Wedge. *Peacemaking Circles: from crime to community*. St. Paul, Minnesota: Living Justice Press, 2003.

Ross, Rupert. *Dancing with a Ghost: exploring Indian reality*. Toronto, Ontario: McClelland and Stewart, Inc., 1992.

_____. *Returning to the Teachings: exploring aboriginal justice*. Toronto, Ontario: Penguin Books, 1996.

Umbreit, Mark S. *et al*. *Victim Meets Offender: the impact of restorative justice and mediation*. Monsey, NY: Criminal Justice Press, 1994.

Van Ness, Daniel and Karen Heetderks Strong. *Restoring Justice*. Cincinnati, OH: Anderson Publishing Company, 1997.

Zehr, Howard. *A New Focus for Crime and Justice:* changing lenses. Scottsdale, PA: Herald Press, 1990.

Zimmerman, Jack and Virginia Coyle. *The Way of Council*. Las Vegas, NV. Bramble Books, 1996.

Related Readings

Arrien, Angeles. *The Four-Fold Way: walking the paths of the warrior, teacher, healer and visionary*. San Francisco, CA: Harper San Francisco, 1993.

Glassman, Bernie. *Bearing Witness: a zen master's lessons in making peace*. New York, NY: Harmony Books, 1998.

Goleman, Daniel. *Emotional Intelligence: why it can matter more than IQ*. New York, NY: Bantam Books, 1995.

Gurian, Michael. *The Wonder of Boys*. New York: Tarcher/Putnam, 1997.

Kessler, Rachael. *The Soul of Education: helping students find connection, compassion and character at school.* Alexandria, VA: Association for Supervision and Curriculum Development, 2000.

Palmer, Parker J. *To Know As We Are Known: education as a spiritual journey*. San Francisco, CA: Harper San Francisco, 1993.

Pipher, Mary. *Reviving Ophelia: saving the selves of adolescent girls*. New York, NY: Ballantine Books, 1994.

Rosenberg, Marshall. *Nonviolent Communication: a language of life*. Encinitas, CA: PuddleDancer Press, 2003.

Related Websites

Evolve.org: www.barbaramarxhubbard.com/con/evolvepage.html

Howard Zehr: www.restorativejustice.org/leading/zehr

International Institute of Restorative Practices: www.iirp.org

Passageworks Institute: www.passageworks.org

reSolutionaries, Inc: www.resolutionariesinc.com

Restorative Justice in Colorado: www.rjcolorado.org

Social Responsibility Inc.: www.socialresponsibilityinc.org

Tom Cavanagh: www.restorativejustice.com/Restorative Justice

Meet the Author

Beverly B. Title, Ph.D. was a public school educator for 21 years and developed one of the first national bullying prevention programs. In 1994 Dr. Title made a career shift and teamed up with Lana Leonard to found Teaching Peace. This nonprofit agency partners with police, courts and  schools to deliver restorative justice services. She stepped down as Executive Director after 14 years, at which time the Board of Directors honored her with the title of Director Emerita. She continues to provide consultation and training at LCJP as well as volunteering with the RATES (restorative alternative to expulsion and suspension) Program.

Dr. Title has presented on restorative justice and provided training in the U.S., Europe and South America, and she has received numerous recognitions throughout her career. She is especially proud of her 2001 Virginia Mackey Award for Leadership in Restorative Justice that was bestowed by the Colorado Forum on Community Restorative Justice.

In 2007 the Colorado legislature created a Restorative Justice Council and Beverly Title was an original appointee where she still serves. She now partners with Kappy Hall at ReSolutionaries, Inc to bring restorative practices to schools and communities.

Beverly and her husband live in Longmont, Colorado, with her daughter, son-in-law and the grandchildren nearby.

ReSolutionaries, Inc.

Providing materials, training and consultation to support the implementation of excellent restorative justice practices in schools and other communities

ReSolutionaries, Inc currently has a series in development of nine posters that teach essential restorative concepts, and the first one is now available. It is a beautifully illustrated version of the graphic on page 169 of this book. Follow our progress and find other products as they become available at www.resolutionariesinc.com.

Order now:

Restorative Practices Create a Context of Care

This beautiful, full color, 18" X 24" poster on high quality paper keeps the restorative message alive in homes, hallways, classrooms and offices — any place where people gather.

Prices:
$8 – 1 to 19 copies
$7 – 20-39 copies
$6 – 40 or more copies
www.reSolutionariesinc.net

Order from: www.resolutionariesinc.com